FLIGHT TEST:
THE DISCIPLINE

"Once you fly, you will

walk with your eyes skyward.

For there you have been

and there you will go again."

– Leonardo da Vinci

FLIGHT TEST:

THE DISCIPLINE

A comprehensive exploration of the
basic tenets of flight test
as a discipline and profession.

Peter Tyson

authorHOUSE®

AuthorHouse™
1663 Liberty Drive
Bloomington, IN 47403
www.authorhouse.com
Phone: 1 (800) 839-8640

Published by AuthorHouse 03/26/2020

ISBN: 978-1-7283-4261-0 (sc)
ISBN: 978-1-7283-4260-3 (e)

Library of Congress Control Number: 2020900323

*This book is dedicated
to the men and women of Flight Test
without them, we would never
have conquered the skies.*

FLIGHT TEST:

THE DISCIPLINE

Table of Contents

List of Figures

About the Authors

Peter Tyson

US Navy helicopter pilot, with 21 years of active duty service. Developmental test pilot; graduate of US Naval Test Pilot School (TPS) in Patuxent River MD, later served as a flight instructor at TPS. Over 3,500 hours of operational and test flight in more than 20 different aircraft. Worked flight test projects for mission systems and air vehicles while at Air Test and Evaluation Squadron TWO ONE (HX-21). Peter gained experience as a program manager and systems engineer for multiple aircraft in two naval aviation programs.

Currently develops and teaches workforce development courses for Naval Air Systems Command (NAVAIR) University; test planning, execution, and reporting for NAVAIR's College of Test and Evaluation (CT&E); sustaining engineering, cybersecurity, and condition-based maintenance for College of Logistics and Industrial Operations (CLIO); critical thinking, risk-based decision making, and project management for College of Program Management (CPM); and training courses for AVIAN Institute. Lead author of **Flight Test: The Discipline**. Owner and founder of P H Tyson & Associates, LLC, dedicated to communication, leadership, and training.

Kevin Switick

US Navy helicopter aircraft commander and Chief OTD. Over 2,200 hours of flight in 40 different aircraft. Designated "Category D" Experimental Test Pilot and former instructor at TPS. Worked on mission systems, air vehicle fly-by-wire flight control systems, and shipboard dynamic interface flight tests. Experienced major acquisition Program Manager (PM) and senior T&E manager for DoD satellite systems and an $11B attack helicopter program.

Currently developer and instructor for NAVAIR University CT&E, CPM, and leadership courses. President and CEO of AVIAN, Inc.

Jeff "Woody" Danielson

US Navy helicopter pilot, TPS graduate, and former flight instructor. Served as the US Navy's Government Flight Test Director (GFTD) and Lead Engineering Test Pilot for the final technical evaluation of the MH-60R Multi-Mission Helicopter. Later served as the senior military test pilot for the US Marine Corps (USMC) Presidential Helicopter Program before completing a 20-year US Navy career, which included a 3-year exchange tour with the Royal Australian Navy.

As a civilian, Woody supported the US Navy for eight years as the lead Project Officer and Unmanned Aerial System (UAS) pilot for the MQ-8 Fire Scout flight test program.

Greg "Gunny" Griffitt

US Navy helicopter pilot, with over 2,700 hours of flight in more than 40 different aircraft. Graduate of the United Kingdom's Empire Test Pilots School. Developmental Test Pilot and Operational Test Director, responsible for T&E of aircraft mission systems, weapons integration, and air vehicle flight test. Part 107 small UAS certified, and part-owner of a counter UAS joint venture.

Author and instructor of two NAVAIR training courses, Operational Test Fundamentals, and T&E Boot Camp. Former AVIAN Vice President for T&E, and Program Manager for the NAVAIR T&E Program Leadership Division support contract supervising more than 85 T&E professionals serving multiple test squadrons and program offices throughout NAVAIR.

Patrick "Oxy" Moran

US Marine Corps fighter pilot who led carrier-based combat sorties in Iraq before becoming a Developmental Test Pilot. Experienced F/A-18 test pilot, TPS flight instructor, and lead government test pilot for US Navy/Marine Corps variants of the F-35 Joint Strike Fighter (JSF).

Oxy served as a deputy program manager and lead systems engineer for the F/A-18 program office. Trained NAVAIR's newest Flight Test Engineers (FTE) in T&E planning, execution, and reporting. Developed and delivered workforce development courses for AVIAN Institute, including **Flight Test: The Discipline** and **Flight Test: Risk Management**, 2-day training courses that accompany this book.

Flight Test: The Discipline

AVIAN Workforce Development & Training Division

Relevant. Tailored. Focused.

http://avian.com

We **believe** that knowledge is power and that we expand knowledge through targeted, meaningful training.

Your future, simplified.

We **base our approach** on the principles of instructional systems design, tailor-made to your specific workforce development and training needs.

To date, AVIAN has created more than 30 customer unique training courses and instructed over 350 classes to over 5,500 students at 14 client sites throughout the United States.

- **Curriculum design and management**
  Tailor-made to your organizational needs, our workforce development curriculum focuses on your processes, your procedures, and your corporate culture.

- **Courseware design and development**
  Our courses are customized to your crucial leadership messages and designed to tell a story—your story. We emphasize the 'so what' and 'why' behind your best practices, not just the 'how.'

- **Course and training materials production**
  Our products are designed to your specifications and made with you, branded for you, and owned by you. They belong to you.

- **Instruction and course delivery**
  Trained in the art of storytelling, our instructors skillfully facilitate learning by engaging your students in thought-provoking discussions. We don't lecture; we have conversations.

P H Tyson & Associates, LLC

If communication is not your top priority, then all your other priorities are at risk.

https://phtyson.com

Effective Workforce Training

In the classroom, during a workshop, or across the lunch table, I explain new concepts and principles with personal examples and anecdotes. I gained my experiences from 21 years as a US Navy Officer, helicopter test pilot, test pilot instructor, program manager, system engineer, and leader. During my career, I spent time on both sides of the classroom, as a student and as an instructor.

From experience, my teaching objectives are simple. They start with making every second in the training room memorable. Then, I make sure that they are enjoyable. Lastly, and perhaps most importantly, I work to create a training environment worthy of the investment of our most precious commodity—our time! I have found that students are open and receptive to new knowledge and skills when not bored or distracted. This observation includes adult learners in the workforce training environment.

My Passion

I enjoy seeing people's reactions when the complicated becomes simple. Additionally, I like it when the forest appears among the trees. Nothing is better than watching the big picture come into focus for a student. I am ready to help others learn.

I look forward to assisting you on your journey to becoming a successful communicator and leader. Follow on LinkedIn or Facebook.

Preface

In 2009, **Leslie Taylor** took a chance. She was the head of Flight Test Engineering at the Naval Air System Command (NAVAIR) in Patuxent River, MD. As the lead civilian for the Flight Test competency (functional area) in a military organization, she saw a deficiency in the professional education and training provided to her subordinates. Leslie Taylor leaned forward, partnered with **Kevin Switick**, a former US Navy helicopter test pilot, and developed both the formal Test & Evaluation (T&E) process and training curricula for NAVAIR.

Before that point, the organizational T&E knowledge was kept safe within the schoolhouse of the US Naval Test Pilot School (TPS). The role of TPS was to train fleet naval aviators (Pilots) and naval flight officers (NFOs) on how to use their **knowledge** of the aircraft, mission, and tactics to become Developmental Test Pilots/NFOs. During a one-year training program, students learned the **skills** and developed their **abilities** to do the demanding T&E job.

As students, we joked that TPS should have been called the "Test Publishing School." It seemed like all we did was write. Test planning and reporting, both heavily reliant on written documentation, are the unglamorous, however, essential parts of the T&E professional's job. We often remarked that while at TPS, we were in class half-a-day, flying for half-a-day, studying for half-a-day, leaving not much time for sleep and family—you get the idea. It is a demanding course, and it consumed all the time and energy one was able to give it.

But for the civilian T&E workforce, there were precious few opportunities to get this training. Only a handful of Flight Test Engineers (FTEs) were able to attend each year along with the active-duty military students. The US Navy Test Pilot School trained the majority of US Navy and US Marine Corps test Pilots/NFOs, along with all US Army helicopter test pilots (called XPs or experimental pilots).

Back to Leslie Taylor's gamble: First, she documented the **Test Planning** (TP) and **Test Reporting** (TR) processes in a way accessible to her civilian workforce. Before this, various instructions, guidebooks, and organizational **best practices** and **lessons learned** contained the test planning and reporting process. Often, those who had attended TPS to disseminate the unwritten processes through on-the-job training to those in the test squadrons without the TPS education.

Second, she directed the implementation of "mandatory" training for over 700 members of the NAVAIR FTE community, spread across 5 test squadrons, 3 test bases, and multiple functional areas. She did this to provide standardization, knowing that each test program is different and requires unique tailoring of the process to achieve the program's goals.

To get this done, Leslie Taylor relied on Kevin Switick, and this is where he excelled. Along with several AVIAN employees, including **Jeff Danielson**, he did triple duty: developing the training materials to simplify the complex processes, translate the detailed requirements, and help to document and solidify a scattered NAVAIR T&E process. Under the guidance and approval of the T&E leadership (which included the Chief Test Pilots and Chief Test Engineers from each of the squadrons), the task took nearly a year to complete.

Soon after the rollout of the new TP and TR training is where I came into the picture. After his initial success with the launch of the training, Kevin needed help. I retired from active duty and went right to work at AVIAN, supporting NAVAIR and teaching TP and TR fulltime. We went from 12 training courses in 2011 to over 40 classes taught in 2012. Then, **Greg Griffitt** joined AVIAN, and he helped carry the load with TR training, as well as Operational Testing and T&E Management courses that AVIAN developed.

We soon learned that there was a hunger for this type of training outside of the walls of the NAVAIR T&E organization. We have taught the classes to logisticians and engineers. We customized the training for numerous government/industry Integrated Test Teams, which include 6 different major aviation contractors. We taught it to USMC personnel at Marine Forces System Command in Quantico, VA, and to Joint Strike Fighter (JSF) personnel at Eglin AFB in FL. The training spread to other navy commands, and eventually to several industry partners who were not associated with military test efforts. And, in one of my favorite venues, I was invited back to TPS to give lead-in training to the new students during their first week at the schoolhouse, providing the "big picture" behind *why* we do *what* we do before they dove into the year-long course on the *how* to do it.

At AVIAN, Kevin gave the task of taking T&E training to industry to **Pat Moran** and me. We started with a clean sheet of paper and used our background and understanding to craft a NAVAIR-style T&E approach. Our extensive range of experience and industry interaction flavored our T&E ideas, but we "demilitarized" them as much as we could. To support what ended up as a 2-day course about the rigors of the T&E profession, we wrote a detailed outline of the T&E process.

We noticed similarities between what we do in T&E with the classic **Scientific Method** and brought that in as the backbone for the discussion. Our collective experience at AVIAN included Navy and Marine Corps, manned and unmanned flight operations, air vehicle and systems testing, rotary-wing and fixed-wing aircraft, land-based and sea-based systems, combat and peacetime. From this background, we fleshed out the chapters in **Flight Test: The Discipline**. We hope that you learn from what we have to share. We used early versions of this book as a student workbook for our 2-day training course of the same name.

There have been numerous others at AVIAN and within NAVAIR who have helped over the years to develop a vibrant workforce training program. Since its humble beginnings in 2009, Leslie Taylor's idea has blossomed into NAVAIR University, which contains Colleges dedicated to all of the functional areas covered by the NAVAIR workforce. One of the core ideas that started with the beginning of TP and TR training is the *color commentator* concept. With this concept, every class taught by an AVIAN facilitator is joined by a senior civilian representative who is intimately familiar with the application of the material to the day-to-day job. I have worked with dozens of these color commentators over the years and indeed have gained tremendous knowledge from them. I could not have done my job without their assistance.

One last comment before we get started: in this book, we give the fundamental concepts in the context of aviation and flight test. However, the same principles, ideas, and processes can apply to all types of T&E, including test and evaluation of cars, appliances, technology, and even something as mundane as a toaster. Design engineering can only take us part of the way to the technology solutions for the problems facing humankind. Ultimately it is the T&E professional, the *evaluation experts*, who are engineers in their own right, who join in the effort and bring products and processes to market, to our businesses, to our homes, and our lives.

Peter Tyson
peter@phtyson.com

Intro to Flight Test

"To design a flying machine is nothing.

To build it is not much.

But to test it is everything."

- Ferdinand Ferber

Intro to Flight Test

The *Discipline* of *Flight Test* is as old as aviation itself. Even before conquering human-crewed, powered flight at Kitty Hawk, unpowered glider flight testing was performed in many places by many individuals for quite some time. Perhaps their exploits and their machines were viewed by those gathered around as a novelty.

The public considered talk of flying as the rantings of crazy men following a crazy dream. Their machines appeared as the awkward, uncoordinated movements of the baby bird hopping along the ground after falling from the nest. But some saw (and caught) the spirit, and understood the power and capability that they were working to unleash.

In 1904, after six years of frustrating glider flight tests reaching a maximum distance of 5 meters, Ferdinand Ferber made the following statement[1] in dedication to Otto Lilienthal (1848-1896); a pioneer of aviation:

> *"To design a flying*
> *machine is nothing.*
> *To build it is not much.*
> *But to test it is everything."*
> - Ferdinand Ferber

Lilienthal had embodied the spirit of flight test, beginning with the start of his experimentation with gliders in 1867 (see Figure 1) through documenting his findings and observations in Birdflight as the Basis of Aviation in 1889.[2]

His significant contributions to the knowledge of heavier-than-air flight were made in Germany, near Berlin, with over 2,000 flights in gliders of his design until his death in 1896, with over 5 hours of accumulated flight time. His flights covered a maximum distance of about 25 meters at first, culminating with flights as long as 250 meters in 1893. His research gathered essential aeronautical data. This data enabled him to design and build a range of gliders, including monoplanes, flapping-wing aircraft, and two biplanes.[3]

In 1894 he built a 15-meter high hill to enable launches into the prevailing wind from any direction, an investment in testing infrastructure made to increase flight capability and uncouple his flight schedule from the prevailing conditions. People would gather to watch his investigation into flight, and he gained notoriety and fame with pictures of him and his flying machines appearing in many popular publications of the time.

Figure 1: Otto Lilienthal, Pioneer of Flight Test

On August 9, 1896, he started a series of flight tests that were to culminate in flights to distances of 250 meters with his glider. On the fourth flight of the day, the craft pitched nose down, and he did not have enough control authority (achieved by shifting his weight) to correct his flight path.

As a result, Otto fell from a height of about 15 meters (50 ft). He fractured the third cervical vertebra and lost consciousness, ultimately dying 36 hours after the initial crash. His reported last words, translated from his native German, were:

"Sacrifices must be made!"[4]
– Otto Lilienthal

His sacrifice, research, and life's work were a significant inspiration for the Wright brothers, who expanded their own aeronautical body of knowledge with glider data and wind tunnel data from experimentation. Their investigations culminated in the first controlled, sustained flight of a powered, heavier-than-air aircraft on December 17, 1903, in Kitty Hawk, North Carolina.

The contributions of Otto Lilienthal, a flight test pioneer, were a necessary step in ushering in the era of human-crewed flight. Through the years, many others have been instrumental in pushing the boundaries of atmospheric flight, in leading the space age with modern metal and composite air vehicles and advanced propulsion technologies, and in developing advanced avionics and sensors with capabilities far beyond anyone's imagination from just a few decades ago.

More recently, Flight Test Engineers (FTE) and operators have explored the incredible world of unmanned aviation with new applications and technologies. They have converted previously manned systems and ideas into unmanned systems and generated new ideas to meet new challenges.

A Case for Planning

A test pilot arrived at his test squadron one morning to be in-formed that they needed him to fly a helicopter to another test base 1.5 hours away. The other base was conducting a ground test and needed to borrow a static aircraft for the day to conduct the test. It seems simple enough, doesn't it?

Upon arrival and check-in with the tower, the crew was directed to proceed to a location on the airfield where a large group of people had gathered. After landing and shut down of the aircraft, the test pilot exited his craft and confidently walked to the wait-ing assembly. After a welcome and numerous excited hand-shakes, the lead test engineer for the day asked him to lower the probe that is used to safely maneuver the aircraft around the flight deck of a ship in high sea state conditions. The blood rushed from the pilot's head. The probe is routinely removed from the aircraft during land operations, and as such, there wasn't one in-stalled that day.

A simple test turned into a $100,000 mistake. The event was scrubbed, and the aircraft was flown home. That one critical detail of the request from one test site to the other was missed in prep-aration for the day's event. Perhaps a proper plan for this support event would have saved some embarrassment. That was the day that the notion of a *Test Support Plan* was born—such a simple idea born from a costly mistake.

The spirit of ingenuity, courage, and discipline continues today in developing and fielding modern instruments of flight. The spirit of test and evaluation has allowed humanity to conquer the atmosphere and enabled a vast spectrum of powered, manned and unmanned, heavier-than-air aircraft and machines to perform transportation, communication, and conquest missions worldwide in various commercial and military functions.

This book introduces the basic tenets of flight test as a discipline and profession. By exploring the efforts required in planning, execution, and documentation, *Flight Test: The Discipline* aids a test team in shaping the basic process, philosophy, and methodology needed to explore the art of the possible in aviation.

In writing this book, I drew from 80 years of flight test experience gained by Naval Aviation. Lessons learned and best practices from the US Naval Air Systems Command (NAVAIR) are found throughout this book.

The essentials of flight test, including test hazard identification and mitigation, are compared with the *Scientific Method*, a time-tested approach to experimentation and evaluation useful in the discussion of aviation systems test and evaluation.

Finally, the book reviews the concepts of Critical Thinking as they apply to the discipline of flight test and the practical application of test planning and test reporting.

The contributing authors have experience as US Navy and Marine Corps Developmental Test (DT) Pilots (both rotary and fixed-wing), TPS instructors, operational evaluation pilots, and aviation program management and systems engineering professionals. Here, *Flight Test: The Discipline* leverages their experience to explain the methodology and approach used to answer development and acquisition questions.

Figure 2: Lockheed Martin F-35 Lightning II Joint Strike Fighter

> **Important to Note:**
>
> Avoid the **"we'll figure it out as we go along"** test mentality at all costs. It should not be confused with the recognized and disci-plined **"fly-fix-fly"** test approach used by experienced testers during the early developmental stages of a system's design.

Fundamentally, we build aviation systems to meet a need, to perform a function, and to satisfy users' requirements. The design process begins with a review of these requirements to inform the design and development of the aviation system. It continues through the application of the systems engineering process to derive detailed design requirements, and on through the process of actual product design.

Once design prototypes are built, developmental FTEs, operators, and DT pilots receive them for test. The test team undertakes the task of determining if the system meets the design specifications. Additionally, they **verify** that the designer's product requirements are built into the systems correctly: *Was the "system built right?"* Importantly, this verification task is not the culmination of the test effort: the next step in the process is to **validate** the system against the real-world system needs for which the system was initially built (i.e., mission need). In this step, the professional flight test team determines whether or not the "right system" has been built, one capable of meeting the user's need in the environment in which they intend to operate it, and can accomplish the tasks that initiated the design effort.

This book describes the events and processes between design and validation, concentrating on the proven steps to successfully conduct flight tests in a **safe, efficient**, and **effective** manner. The first of these principles, **safe**, is essential to promote the development of the system.

If the test team performs the test in a reckless, *"we'll figure it out as we go along"* manner, the impact of a flight incident may prove to be disastrous for the overall program. Specifically, the loss of a test asset may dramatically impact the cost and schedule of the development,

> **Expensive Test Article:**
>
> The US Marine Corps spent over $50M and 6 months to fully instrument their MV-22 test article.

requiring a replacement asset as well as considerable effort to resume the test program, while attempting to recover and overcome the events that led to the mishap. More importantly, such a cavalier approach to test may lead to injury or loss of life.

For unique one-of-a-kind test articles, the loss of the air vehicle and associated instrumentation may not be replaceable within the program's resource constraints. The time required to resume the testing may become a limiting factor, as investors and sponsors become hesitant to devote effort in pursuit of a system that has not shown returns. Thus the cost of a mishap (including the real dollar cost resulting from the loss of a test asset) may make a recovery of the development program impossible. The time and money required to construct a fully-instrumented test article may rival the entire developmental budget, and the loss of such an investment may cause program leadership to reconsider the entire value proposition and approach to the development effort.

The loss of life or test asset has a dramatic impact on the cost and schedule of the development program, requiring a replacement asset, retraining of a new crew, as well as considerable effort to resume the test program and overcome the events that led to the mishap.

Figure 3: North American XB-70A Valkyrie

Flight Test: The Discipline

Aviation history is replete with "good ideas" that did not reach fruition due to test-related failures and setbacks, such as the North American XB-70A. In this case, the experimental work in supersonic aerodynamics was cut short in part by the flight test crash of one of the two prototypes on June 8, 1966.

The crash occurred during a photoshoot opportunity in a formation of five aircraft powered by General Electric engines (XB-70A, F-4, F-5, T-38, and F-104). After the photoshoot, the XB-70A and F-104 collided and destroyed both aircraft resulting in the death of the F-104 pilot, NASA Chief Test Pilot Joe Walker, the XB-70A co-pilot Carl Cross, and injuring the XB-70A pilot Al White who sustained serious injuries during the ejection.[5]

The hard lessons from *dissimilar* formation, often required during developmental test flights, have been relearned time and time again with bad results, and serve as an example of the risks often considered during test flight planning and execution. Flight test is an unforgiving business, one that requires **discipline**.

Incidents such as these have shaped flight test discipline, now fashioned to consider the hazards inherent to flight and flight test carefully. A significant element of flight test discipline is the concept of risk management. Flight test professionals apply risk management principles with the express aim of eliminating or controlling hazards and preventing the loss of aircraft assets and human life.

The US Navy learned the importance of flight test discipline during the development of the F/A-18 Hornet. While conducting safe separation tests to verify the controlled jettison of a weapon along with the launcher rack from under the left-wing of the Hornet, the released store/rack combination exhibited unpredictable and unsteady aerodynamic qualities. Instead of falling away clear of the aircraft, the assembly tumbled and drifted up in the wake, slicing through the right-wing of the photo chase TA-4 Skyhawk.[6]

The chase aircraft pilot was balancing the needs of two competing requirements. First, get the data, i.e., be as close as possible to allow the photographer in the rear cockpit the best view of the underside of the Hornet's wing to capture essential evidence during the release sequence. Second, fly safely in *dissimilar* formation on a larger aircraft, with proper separation and consideration of the wake turbulence behind and below the Hornet.

Due to multiple lapses in flight test discipline, including process and judgment errors (e.g., improper formation visual references, failure to clear the area before release, consideration of alternate instrumentation techniques), the Skyhawk was in precisely the wrong place at precisely the wrong time during the test event.

Both crewmembers escaped the stricken chase aircraft before it crashed. Still, the lesson of how to properly respect, identify, and mitigate flight-test-related safety hazards was burned indelibly into the US Navy's approach to flight test.

Another aim of the flight test discipline is not as visible but is equally vital to the success of a test program—to

collect flight test data *efficiently*. Deliberate, quality planning and professional execution ensure that the test team performs their test in the most resource conservative way. Test points cost money and time. Thus, the team must prioritize and gather their data carefully, with consideration to value and impact.

After completing a test program for one of the MH-60R sensors, we analyzed the program's cost. The expenses included test range, fuel, maintenance, and operations. We then divided the total cost by the number of test cycles performed. Each test cycle was about 15 minutes long. The resulting cost per cycle was about $60,000

Figure 4: Lockheed Martin MH-60R Seahawk

Had we known that before the start of the program, the sponsor would have undoubtedly wanted assurance that we would plan and execute a flight test with the minimum number of cycles required, without any "extras" or make-up flights.

The final principle inherent to flight test discipline is to design and perform *effective* test programs. To find at the end of an otherwise successful test flight that the data gathered is either meaningless or not suitable for analysis is disheartening to the test team. Re-flights, delays, and missed opportunities are often the result of a rush to fly, without adequate planning and critical thinking informing the test program.

Another danger that faces successful and effective flight test is the natural tendency of the FTE to get distracted in the details of discovery and lose focus on the aim of the test. For example, if the test objective was to find the best route and start time for the car trip from home to work and back again each day, the curious engineer may get wholly absorbed and enthralled by the issue of the flat tire encountered during one of the test trials.

Then the eager engineer may divert the investigation into exploring the best way to avoid getting a flat (and upon getting one how to correct the problem). Soon, the creeping scope of the effort completely consumes scarce test resources (schedule and funding). However, the necessary data to support conclusions and recommendations regarding the route to work (forget the best time of day!) was never collected, and the test essentially becomes a failure.

The three elements of *safe*, *efficient*, and *effective* do not appear in a **Test Plan** by accident. They are fundamental elements and form the cornerstone of the test plan.

The test organization deliberately contemplates these three elements as it works through the steps of the test planning process. With these elements incorporated, the test plan becomes a tool for critical thinking. It is the framework which guides the application of a deliberate thought process as the plan for the test is formulated and presented, ready for others to read and understand.

Building on this foundation, the test execution process follows an orderly flow through the test event, with known roles and responsibilities for each member of the test team. Finally, the culmination of the test effort is the **Test Report**, presenting test results, providing analysis, and the decision-quality data to consider in light of end-user expectations and needs, assembled into a logical and easy to understand format.

The Test Report is complete with the presentation of conclusions and recommendations to decision-makers, offering insight to inform on how to proceed with the end goal of delivering new or improved capability to the customer and end-user.

This book intends to increase your knowledge and enhance your understanding of the flight test discipline to support the safe conduct of efficient and effective flight tests.

Doing this requires a better understanding of aircraft operations and flight test, often gained through discussions of best practices, drawn from both military and commercial flight test, and from discussions intended to increase general awareness of the rigors of flight test.

Flight Test Basics

"The genius is in making

the complex simple."

– Albert Einstein

Flight Test Basics

Before moving to the particular requirements and peculiarities of flight test, a review of the other types of test add necessary context. Flight test is part of a continuum during development, starting with simple *laboratory testing* or *bench testing* of subassemblies and prototypes of portions of the final system.

Information from this testing is inserted back into the design process, a feedback loop providing rapid, essential performance and technical data for the designer – who may be the one performing the test. The lab or bench test takes many forms and uses many representations of the final system, including mockups, breadboards, and prototypes. External inputs and some internal components may be simulated or virtual. Laboratory or bench tests become more in-depth and complicated as the system nears completion and full integration of all the components. Different types of lab or bench tests include:

1. Software module tests
2. Environmental/climatic chamber tests
3. Material properties tests
4. Vulnerability/survival tests
5. Static engineering tests
6. Dynamic engineering tests

Many of the demonstrations shown on the TV series *MythBusters* are mostly lab or bench mockups of a concept or idea.[8] The show's stars create a simulation of the *myth*, complete with stand-in body parts, replicas, and models. They carefully present angles, scaled distances, and physics of the *myth* in their simulation.

Armed with data from workshop modeling, they proceed to the next step, a full-size test. Often they mitigate risk and avoid disaster by using mockups or crash-test dummies. But often they subject their bodies to the *myth's* conditions and forces involved—part of the draw for the viewer and fun that the show offers.

Similarly, aviation system development eventually graduates from lab and bench into full *ground testing* of the completed system, bringing together the overall system design and the interfaces among the subsystems.

The aim of ground test includes a fit check (physical size and weight), system power-up (electrical power and cooling requirements), compatibility (interface, communication, standards compliance), and integration (interaction with other systems).

Flight Test: The Discipline

Even though the initial flight test system may not be complete with all the final intended capability, its first flights are done with the minimum ability to *aviate*, even if for a short duration, unsustainable flight.

As confidence and performance grows, the system adds additional ability to *navigate* and *communicate*, the other two primary functions required for controlled, purposeful flight.

Incidentally, the evolutionary addition of system capability while in the test often results in a phased, multi-step test program. These phases add complexity and must be considered during test planning to ensure that we correctly evaluate the capability in the proper context with proper expectations.

Additionally, the purpose of *regression testing* becomes important: to verify that previously evaluated and documented performance remains intact during the addition of new capability (or correction of previously discovered issues). The need for regression tests can rapidly explode the scope (duration, cost) of a test program. If not adequately accounted for early in test planning, regression tests can expand the scope beyond that initially envisioned (or budgeted).

Back to the minimum capability required for the first ground or flight tests: in this context, *aviate* describes the action of moving through the air, powered or unpowered, but sustained and stable. The system must then be able to *navigate* or maneuver through the air from one location to another to move in a controlled fashion (the next step in the evolution of the design).

Finally, *communicate* means more than the rudimentary two-way exchange of words between the operator and a ground controller with a radio. It also includes completing a useful function or mission employment of a sensor, transportation of an object, or transfer of information.

From this, we discover the end goal of flight test: more than just the ability to move or control movement through the air but to perform the desired task. It is only in the context of this task/mission that the flight test becomes an actual flight evaluation to determine the usefulness of the system in achieving the desired effect.

The flight test and design engineers must collaboratively conduct a determination of readiness to leap into the air before commencing a flight test program. Typically this is referred to as a **Test Readiness**

Review (TRR) or a **Flight Readiness Review** (FRR), where participants examine the merits of the system's design, review the preparations for flight tests, and agree upon the overall test approach.

Entry into flight test (through the gatekeeper TRR or FRR process) requires the rigor and standardization demonstrated during requirements generation, decomposition, and integration process (i.e., the system engineering design process) step up to the next level. It is, in essence, a *deliberate* **critical thinking** event. An opportunity for the design team and test team to slow down and think critically about what they are about to do.

The fundamental methods, characteristics, and philosophy of the discipline of flight tests are universal throughout the industry. However, the unique requirements brought forth in every test program lead to the tailoring of the processes.

In other words, the TRR or FRR, even if called by a different name and following a different step-by-step process or checklist, examines the same questions:

- *Have all the necessary steps been completed to ensure that the system is ready for its first flight ever?*

- *Or the first flight in this configuration?*

- *Or the first flight under these conditions?*

Levels of Flight Test

No flight test is routine; instead, some change or update in the design of the system under consideration initiates the need. Invariably, flight test involves an element of discovery. As the system evolves from drawing board to flight, tests learn about the design implications and discover its uniqueness.

Initially, the flight tests determine whether the system works as designed: how faithful to the drawings, design, and intent. Later, the testing shifts to learning how well the system can work and under what controlled conditions will it perform as desired. Finally, the testing explores how well it works under a variety of conditions that match those expected to be encountered in the intended operational environment when used in a representative way.

Thus, the purpose of flight test moves through four distinct phases: first *Discovery*, then *Verification*, on to *Characterization*, and finally *Validation*. We perform these phases against the contextual backdrop of the intended task or mission of the system. Here are the four levels of flight test:

1. **Discovery**
   What are the design features, and do they work as intended? Are there inherent limitations to the design to be addressed immediately?

2. **Verification**
   Compare the design to the drawings/specification. *Does the system match the design intent?*

3. **Characterization**
   Document the performance obtained or obtainable within the design, system capabilities, and design limitations for later use in the Owner's Manual.

4. **Validation**
   Is the design the right one for the purpose? Does it properly operate in its intended environment? Does it meet the needs of the end-user?

Four Levels of Flight Test

Discovery–does it work?

Verification–is it built according to the design?

Characterization–how does it work and what does it do?

Validation–is it the right design for the mission?

To achieve its purpose, the demands of flight test discipline require that the test combines the correct knowledge with the right perspective. The perspective lenses required are that of the designer and the operator.

First, the **engineering approach**—seeing theory, principles, and mechanics at work in the design's simplicity, complexity, and elegance.

Second, the **practical approach** of the operator—who desires effectiveness in accomplishing the task and suitability for use.

We use both perspectives to assess: (1) the system under test, (2) the design mission, and (3) the intended environment in which it operates.

Detailed knowledge/understanding of these three items is necessary to test the system under test properly, with the following characteristics of flight test:

1. *Safe* for both man and machine.

2. *Efficient* in time and resources.

3. *Effective* at gathering the data for the analysis to arrive at a meaningful answer.

The engineering approach described above deserves a little more discussion. There are different levels of understanding of the system (or software), each with advantages and disadvantages that help facilitate the test. This concept, borrowing from software engineers, starts with *black box*, the **first level** of knowledge.

Black box describes the condition where the tester does not know the inner works of the system or software. What is known are the inputs required and outputs expected of the fully-functioning system or component. Therefore, we construct a test to simulate (or stimulate) the proper input conditions and verify that the system produces correct (and useful) outputs. We are of little help when the outputs do not match expectations. In this case, the tester can only verify that they reached the right input conditions and documented the results.

A difficulty of *black box* is that the tester is at the mercy of the designer in knowing how the system produced the output and what impacts errors or design accuracy (tolerances) have on the overall capability. With *black box* testing, the test team can consist of test technicians who follow a *recipe* or step-by-step test procedure written by the design engineer. Tests of this type are sometimes called *acceptance tests*.

The second level of knowledge, *white box*, reveals the inner workings of the system under test to the FTE. They see the data flow through the inside of the "box" and can look for the cause if the result is not correct. They understand the error stack up through the system and see how the system impacts the overall capability in more ways than merely producing desired outputs given a set of inputs.

Also, the tester can craft *white box* tests with a meaningful spread of conditions. This ability allows for the assessment of "corner" and "edge" cases that were unknown to the tester in the *black box* test.

However, *white box* testing comes at a cost. The team typically requires training and time to absorb the design and to understand concepts. The time allows them to apply critical thought during test execution to capture and verify the system's design thoroughly.

The test program may take much longer than with a *black box* approach and appear less efficient. But this may be worth the trade, as the *white box* approach enables the team to improve on the design and plan for test specific hazards in ways that they cannot with *black box*. However, the team may lose objectivity if they become too familiar with the *how* of the system design. The detailed knowledge may cloud their assessment of *if* it works.

The *white box* approach is even more effective if the test team applies their real-world experience using similar types of systems in the intended operational environment. The need for relevant experience is one reason why test pilots must have a minimum number of operational flight hours before they begin training to be test pilots; to come armed with that first-hand operational knowledge and experience.

Black box
Unknown inner workings,
but defined inputs have expected outputs

White box
In-depth knowledge of interior processes and flow,
understanding of error sources and tolerances

Gray box
Hybrid approach combining benefits of white and black

The **third level** of knowledge is a hybrid of the first two: *gray box* testing combines the advantages of both. Tailored depth of knowledge, based on the sensitivity of the overall performance to the different subroutines, logic paths, or networks inside the box gives the tester a deep *white box* level of knowledge in critical areas that impact safety, efficiency, or effectiveness of the test.

This knowledge can help the tester improve the system's design during the test. Other areas that are well-established, routine, or not critical to mission success or safety are considered *black box*.

Segregating portions of the test effort into *black box* and *white box* streamlines the time and effort required to get into the test program, set the configuration and conditions, measure the results, and compare to the expected output or a notion of the mission needs.

For example, when testing avionics software: for the data flow and path of navigation information to align sensors, calibrate antennae, or perform another mission-related function, the tester may use the *black box* approach and proceed without in-depth knowledge of the inner workings of the software.

However, the position and state information from the same inertial navigation system may require *white box* knowledge. If that information contributes to critical flight control functions (such as autopilot, attitude/airspeed hold, or altitude maintenance), the test team must have detailed knowledge of the signal path, error budgets, and algorithms to test and evaluate properly. Thus the overall navigation system may be considered *gray box* testing.

The Goal of Flight Test

The goal of flight test is to arrive at meaningful answers to questions about the system, its design, operations, and capabilities. When viewed through the eyes of the tester, the system reveals characteristics about itself piece-by-piece as *data*, carefully observed, measured, and recorded by the test team.

Coherent *information* is created from the raw data as test results indicate system performance, capability, and response. The information helps the team build their *knowledge* about how the system performs during tests and functions under various anticipated operational conditions.

Assessing knowledge against an understanding of the design and operational intent of the system, mission, and environment allows the test team to generate *insight* regarding decisions to be made in the development of the system.

This insight (or wisdom) can be translated and communicated to the designer, manager, user, or operator through several formal and informal test reporting means, to permit insightful and informed *decisions*.

The path of data-to-decision from flight test can be broken or interrupted in many ways, but many of the barriers coalesce simply to test cost and test schedule. First, the cost or the resources required to stress the system, stimulate the system, or provide the system with the right environment to collect the data may be a limiting factor.

Secondly, the time required to obtain sufficient data to generate the information, knowledge, and wisdom required to inform the

---

Good, Fast, Cheap. Pick Two.

A commonly expressed mantra of the flight test discipline is *"you can have it fast, you can have it cheap, or you can have it good—but you can only have two of the three—which two do you want?"*

Sometimes all the customer needs at a certain point in a program is a fast and cheap answer to make a programmatic decision (e.g., a cost, schedule, performance trade), and that's ok.

decision-maker may be a barrier. Often managers or sponsors of the test must balance the quality, quantity, or confidence in the test results conveyed through the report against the time and money available for the test.

To determine the required level of confidence needed for a flight test, the test team must understand the nature of the decision and the position or role of the audience.

- The design engineer may be interested in a rough order-of-magnitude answer to facilitate initial design choices.
- Senior-level management may need to understand the viability of technological approaches to determine where to invest.
- Program and project managers may need to verify requirement compliance for contract adjudication or for under-standing, which cost, schedule, and performance trades to make.
- Or, other T&E professionals want visibility in the test progress, methodology, and lessons learned to inform similar, parallel, or subsequent efforts on the same or follow-on systems.

Not only does understanding the audience's point of view help the tester calibrate the quest for knowledge and wisdom in the flight test program, but it also helps to set the tone and the voice in the report.

All readers want to understand the "*So What?*" and the "*What needs to be done?*" from the test results. The writer must correctly understand the audience to be able to provide the right level of detail and the appropriate amount of underlying background material. Only by knowing the audience can the writer adequately address the urgency of the recommended response in the test report.

The audience members have different needs from the outcome of the flight test; different understanding of the system capabilities, limitations, and design; and different expectations from the test team and what they deliver as an answer to the initial question or questions that prompted the flight test program in the first place.

Pillars of Flight Test Success

Successful flight test relies upon 3 pillars: (1) people, (2) resources, and (3) procedures. Knock out one of these three pillars, and the overall flight test collapses in a heap with no tangible results.

The **first pillar** is people who must be trained, designated, and current. The first of these three, training, means that they must possess the requisite **knowledge**, **ability**, and **skill** (KAS) to perform the flight test tasks asked of them.

Knowledge
May be gained from study, classroom, and experience. Exposure to the terms, definitions, and facts of the flight test discipline assist flight test engineers greatly in the critical analysis required to perform flight tests. They learn from all phases of the test process. For example, they learn from the deliberate discussion and analysis during the test planning and reporting phases.

Additionally, participating in real-time decision making during test execution and data collection builds foundational knowledge for future tests. Finally, exposure to the time-critical reactions required when seconds are the only thing between success and failure provides the flight test engineer with valuable knowledge and experience.

Ability
It comes through practice and repetition. Experience from past encounters with similar issues guide the decision-making process. With ability comes the unconscious linkage of learned knowledge to practical application, occasionally expressed as *"following a gut feel"* rapidly followed up with logical and methodical reasoning. Within one's demonstrated ability, the science and art of flight test join together.

Skill
Superior knowledge and ability in a particular area of effort. It is in the demonstrated skill of flight test that one earns a reputation for excellence, performance, and success. Those in the organization that have flight test skill are living out a quote from Vince Lombardi, as it would apply to the discipline of flight test:

Knowledge
may be gained from
study and classroom

Ability
develops with practice
and repetition

Skill
is recognized superior
knowledge and ability

"The quality of a person's life is in direct proportion to their commitment to excellence, regardless of their chosen field of endeavor."
- Vince Lombardi

Skill in flight test requires an absolute commitment to excellence, a dedication to the discipline, and an understanding/ mastery of fundamental principles and processes inherent to flight test. **Knowledge** is the foundation, **ability** is the discipline, and **skill** is excellence.

However, ability and skill do not follow from knowledge just because one is repeatedly doing flight test tasks, which serves to highlight a Vince Lombardi quote regarding practice, repetition, and perfection:

"Practice does not make perfect. Perfect practice makes perfect."
- Vince Lombardi

Flight Test: The Discipline

Members of the test team must not only have the requisite **knowledge**, **ability**, and **skill** to support the task; they should have a designation and approval to function in their roles. Designation formally recognizes the KAS of a team member.

The designation process may be an essential part of a large team with many simultaneous test efforts, but not as crucial for a small team where team member roles, responsibilities, and positions are otherwise known.

Regardless of formal designation, team members must have one final quality: they must be current in their exercise of flight test KAS. Their experience must be up to date and relevant to the systems they test.

The **second pillar** for flight test success involves the resources needed for the test. Therefore, it starts with a **plan** (more to follow) that is an approved, ready-to-execute summation of the critical thinking and process for execution of the test.

First Pillar: People

They must have the requisite KAS.

They must be designated (formally recognized).

They must have current/relevant experience.

They must be available for the test and ready!

Secondly, the *pilots* and *operators* for the system must be in sync with the flight test engineers. They must be on the same sheet of music, ready to participate, and contribute toward test success.

The primary means to accomplish synchronization of the test team's effort is through the **Test Plan**, and secondarily through a thorough and meaningful pre-event briefing and post-event debrief.

Facilities

This resource includes hangars for preparation, storage, maintenance, and safekeeping of the system. Facilities represent the external resources required for a flight test program. They must be scheduled and coordinated. The test team must understand the resources available: power, communication, storage, floor space, and offices.

Ground support equipment (GSE)

Must be obtained, serviced, and readied for use to maintain the aircraft (or system under test). Often overlooked: the test team must check calibration dates, deconflict dual-use with other organizations, and perform servicing (especially for seldom-used gear in disrepair).

Instrumentation

Must be installed, checked, and calibrated. Test plan writers must consider the impact of the instrumentation on the system, for both the airworthiness and data integrity.

The **third pillar** for flight test success includes documented ground and flight test procedures, and the processes in place to govern the conduct of the test.

Standard Operating Procedures

Sometimes they are called Squadron Operating Procedures (SOP). Still, either way, they are used throughout industry and the military to provide leadership's direction when faced with defined conditions: *"if this happens, perform this action,"* or *"if given these conditions, act in this way."*

Second Pillar: Resources

They must be coordinated.

They must be scheduled.

They must be prepared.

They must be available for the test and ready!

System Training

Another critical tenet of the flight test discipline is ensuring the thorough training of the flight test pilots and aircrew on the system's design. Insufficient system training can cause significant test program delays and schedule slips.

A classic example comes from the introduction of a new system (shown in Figure 5) to replace a legacy system. The system was an underwater transducer array (sonar) designed to be lowered beneath a hovering helicopter into the ocean and used to detect and track submarines. The legacy system had 4 modes of opera-tion; the new system had 12: the original 4 plus 8 new modes. As the test pilots and aircrew were not sufficiently trained on the purpose and use of the 8 new modes, during the test, they concentrated on the 4 legacy modes, the ones with which they were most familiar.

As a result, the reports coming out of the test stated that the new $1M system upgrade showed no significant performance enhancement over the legacy system, and the program was nearly canceled.

Once the training error was identi-fied and corrected, and the proper use of the new modes incorpo-rated into the test execution, the test data showed a 3x perfor-mance enhancement. Do not un-dervalue the training tenet— system training needs to be con-ducted by the design engineer who understands the nuances, advantages, and intent of the complete design.

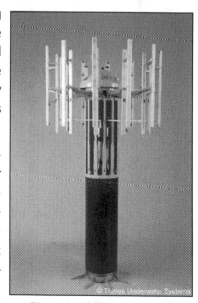

Figure 5: Thales Advanced Low-Frequency Sonar (ALFS) Transducer Array

---

Third Pillar: Process

They must be standardized.

They must be documented.

They must promote understanding and compliance.

They must be up-to-date and enforced!

Although the SOP cannot cover all scenarios and circumstances, a well-designed SOP provides guidance and insight into intent that helps the team understand their limits of authority and responsibility.

Test Plan

In addition to the general coverage of the SOP, the test team needs to have an approved test plan. This crucial document serves as specific authorization and coverage for the actions involved in the test.

Configuration Management (CM)

Combining the test plan with a functioning CM program allows the team to have an accurate understanding of the system under test, critical in a fast-paced development program with both routine and urgent changes to the design integration.

The test team must follow the SOP, test plan, and CM documents in the face of internal and external pressure to "cut corners" or bypass what they contain. The author wrote the documents for a reason; however, all things are indeed negotiable. An SOP can be altered or modified to deal with unique situations, but can only be done by one with authority to do so (typically the author/signer or their delegate).

The test team should be vigilant against violating the CM process. Shortcuts and bypasses to proper CM not only have safety implications (worst case) but often impact test effectiveness. The loss of effectiveness comes from inconsistent results, which undercut the analysis of the data and the ability to make conclusions from the test.

The Scientific Method and Flight Test, Part I

"Science, my boy,

is made up of mistakes,

but they are mistakes

which it is useful to make,

because they lead little by little

to the truth."

– Jules Verne

Journey to the Center of the Earth

The Scientific Method and Flight Test, Part I

The scientific method has been used for centuries to guide experimentation and exploration and has been instrumental in the development of theories and descriptions of the natural world around us. Additionally, the scientific method is a framework for the discovery and analysis of human-made systems. The process of flight test is closely related to the scientific method (see Figure 6), and provides a basis for the discussion of flight test that follows.

Before exploring parallels between flight test and the scientific method, it helps to know some background for the method. The origins of the modern scientific method can be traced back as far as the early history of Egypt in medical discussions (c. 1600 BC), through Chinese writings describing a methodology for testing truth or falsehood of statements (c. 400 BC), and on to the Greek philosophers contemplating the descriptions of abstract concepts and ideas (c. 400-200 BC).[9]

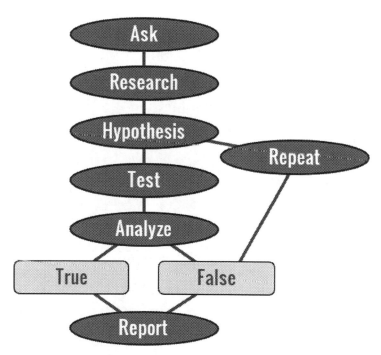

Figure 6: The Scientific Method

However, the particular formulation used here is closer to the experimental methodology first discussed by the Persian scientist, mathematician, astronomer, and philosopher Hasan Ibm alHaytham (Alhazen). He championed the concept that the experimenter must prove the hypothesis through experimentation based on the principles of evidence.

Alhazen documented this methodology in his seven-volume treatise, Book of Optics around 1020 AD, approximately 200 years before Renaissance scientists furthered his ideas.[10]

During the Renaissance, an Englishman named Roger Bacon described the scientific method in his *Opus Majus* (1267 or 1268 AD), inspired by Aristotle and Alhazen.

"[T]heories supplied by reason should be verified by sensory data, aided by instruments, and corroborated by trustworthy witnesses."[11]

– Roger Bacon

While there is no one formulation of the scientific method, most descriptions include the necessary steps described here. The discussion in Wikipedia provides insight equally applicable to flight test.[12]

Scientific Method

"The scientific method is not a single recipe: It requires intelligence, imagination, and creativity. In this sense, it is not a mindless set of standards and procedures to fol-low, but is rather an ongoing cycle, constantly develop-ing more useful, accurate, and comprehensive models and methods."

– Wikipedia Contributors

Step 1. The Need for Flight Test

The scientific method begins with asking a question. Typically in an experiment, the question starts with "Why?" The question may address something observed in the natural world that the experimenter is attempting to duplicate. Or the question may address the need to understand the mechanism and workings behind the result.

In the advancement of new technology, development of new systems, or evaluation of the utility of an air vehicle with integrated systems intended to perform a mission or task, the question is a little different.

"Is this a viable technology to address the need?" The demonstration of a new technology is vital to directing the overall developmental effort. First, understanding the feasibility of alternatives and then determining the best course of action are two direct results from the data gained during the test.

In demonstrations, the final desired capability is not the aim. Instead, most demonstrations focus on a portion of the overall end product. Perhaps the key ingredient to making a sensor work (optics, timing, or receptor) or the approach to defying the law of gravity (rotors, fans, jets, wings, displacement) is the focus.

For example, the technology challenge for the F-35 Joint Strike Fighter (JSF) came from the US Marine Corps. The USMC required a Short Take-Off Vertical Landing (STOVL) capability, which for a 5th generation fighter, was no easy task.

As an aside, "Joint" in this context means two or more services combining their efforts into one

---

Experiment vs. Test

The basic difference between an experiment and a test:

In an *experiment*, the scientist is trying to discover the answer to an unanswered question and prove the hypoth-esis true or false.

In a *test*, the tester has a question with a projected answer (prediction) from the design engineer, obtained through engineering analysis or modeling and simulation (M&S), and the test engineer is trying to verify and/or validate it.

program. Therefore the USMC STOVL requirement was in tension with the US Air Force (land-based) and US Navy (carrier-based) takeoff and landing requirements, all for the same aircraft design. That ultimately led to three variants of the "one" JSF.

For the USMC STOVL variant, two contractors provided unique solutions to the government: (1) a lift jet using hot thrust from the engine only or (2) a combination of lift jet and a "cold" lift fan.

Two separate test programs commenced, each to demonstrate the capability of a unique technological approach. In what essentially created a side-by-side comparison (or "fly-off") to view the pros and cons of the two technologies, program managers selected the best approach (from a cost, schedule, and performance perspective).

They ended up picking the technology that used a lift fan, one with a 90° gearbox and a clutch used to transfer 29,000 shaft horsepower from the main engine to the LiftFan, an incredible technical achievement!

Another example of a technology demonstration involved the use of a novel underwater detection method: blue-green lasers. The laser system provided visibility in a murky environment, the turbid shallow water of the littoral oceans.

Here, the system's task was to find, target, and neutralize submerged sea mines, which were a threat to safe navigation. Design engineers created a system to shoot the mines with a *supercavitating* bullet capable of penetrating the water.

For this technology demonstration, a known air vehicle provided a stable air platform (AH-1W Cobra helicopter). A 25-year old laser from a previous program was added to the aircraft to provide target illumination.

Also, the Cobra's gun was replaced by another Gatling gun system, borrowing proven technology from another aircraft, the F/A-18 Hornet. The gun barrels were hand-selected for accuracy during multiple ground firing-tunnel tests. A fire control system related to that used on a shipboard defense Gatling gun provided control of the gun.

The final pieces of the system comprised: purpose-built software, a highly sensitive photoreceptor and processor to capture the reflected laser energy, and a one-of-a-kind cockpit control/display system. The photoreceptor processor was the new piece of technology, and the critical questions we asked were:

Is the sensor fast enough to differentiate between the reflected laser pulse from the water's surface and the second, smaller return from the mine?

And, if the sensor accurately determined the timing of the two pulses from inside a hovering helicopter outside of the potential blast radius, would the fire control system be able to compute the depth of the target?

Considering Snell's Law and the refraction of light through the air-water interface, the problem was complex.

We did not know if the gun was accurate enough to target a submerged mine and deliver enough energy into it with a direct hit from a single bullet.

Even if it hit, would the blow from the supercavitating bullet have enough energy to render the mine harmless?

Based on the findings of the demonstration, within the limitations of the cobbled-together system, decisions could be made about whether to invest resources into a new, bottom-up design of hardware and software using this new technology.

"What are the limitations of this technology?" Are there boundaries within which the technology may work? The investigation centers on safely determining the application of the technology and learning the trade space that exists for the design. Undesirable characteristics and by-products of the approach are defined and evaluated for improvement, often at the cost of giving up some desired ability or performance.

Figure 7: Bell AH-1W Cobra

Figure 8: Bell/Boeing V-22 Osprey

Design tradeoffs have always been a factor for the Vertical/Short Take-off and Landing (V/STOL)[13] technology. Throughout years of development, designers have used many approaches in an attempt to reach a viable solution.[14]

Early Developmental Test and Evaluation (DT&E) of the Bell/Boeing V-22 Osprey tilt-rotor focused on the trade space between *effective* vertical flight (helicopter mode) and *efficient* horizontal flight (aircraft mode). Maximizing the cargo-carrying capability (gross weight) versus speed and range were essential to making the revolutionary change to aviation history.

"Does the solution provided by the vendor or designer meet the requirements?" *Verification* of the design against the requirements is an essential part of DT. If a vendor provides the system under test, verification is called *acceptance* test, often with contractual implications. The program manager requires data about the system performance to determine if the contractual obligations are complete.

If the organization that designed and built the system conducts the test, it is called *Contractor* DT&E (or simply, CT), performed before final delivery. Contractor DT&E is not performed by the organization that is ultimately going to put the system into operational use. Thus, *verification* activity is different than *characterization* and *validation*.

"Does the system meet the needs of the end-user?" Here test centers on operating a production system in the intended environment, in the anticipated way (tactically), and by a representative of the end-user. *Validation* tests of this nature are called an *Operational* Test (OT). When OT includes verification and characterization along with *validation*, then the combination is called DT/OT (or *Combined DT/OT*).

For military applications, the distinction between CT, DT, and OT is of primary importance, for typically the military does not engage in the full spectrum of design and integration (production) of a system but instead buys the capability from the aerospace industry. With this scheme, industry performs CT, specialized organizations within the military perform DT, and a separate, independent organization (such as the US Navy's Commander, Operational Test Forces, COTF) performs OT.

For an organization that is defining the requirements, designing the system, producing the system, and ultimately operating the system (without distinction between separate companies performing the different functions), the differences between separate CT, DT, and OT may be immaterial. However,

knowledge of the differences is essential in understanding the different perspectives, approaches, and methodologies involved in designing and executing the flight test process.

"Does the system meet a Key Requirement as expressed by the user?" This question is a subset of the previous question (whether the system meets the user's needs). Often specific Key Performance Parameters (KPP) have been developed that describe significant characteristics of the system, without which the utility of the system is dubious.

In daily life, these KPPs take the form of specific requirements when contemplating the purchase of items such as a car for the family (minimum number of passengers) or a house (minimum number of rooms). There is no reason to pursue or investigate a car or house that does not provide these basic features.

In aviation, these can be items such as cruising speed or altitude for an air vehicle, detection range and resolution for a sensor, or endurance and information throughput for a communication or control platform.

Although unverified and potentially apocryphal, the story of approach speed for the US

Navy's carrier-based F-14 Tomcat fighter serves to illustrate. Planners determined the maximum landing approach speed requirement based on the concept of operation for the jet, the current and future anticipated carrier capability, and a large body of knowledge regarding safe, repeatable, and reliable operations from a carrier.

The US Navy was not interested in buying and fielding a new aircraft unless it met this requirement (it was a mandatory requirement). During development, the program officer financially incentivized landing. For every knot of airspeed below the stipulated maximum, the contract awarded an incentive to the manufacturer—a million dollars per knot!

Therefore, at the appropriate time during the development of the aircraft, a flight test was required to ascertain the actual landing speed upon which all parties could agree. The story follows that the test was designed and executed to determine the speed, and the pressure for the flight team to determine the final number must have been enormous!

The test team's methodology would be subject to discussion and dissection, where every knot of speed could potentially be the subject of debate and lawsuit. Understanding the situation, understanding the perspectives of the different stakeholders, and understanding the objectives were essential to the test.

Step 2. The Rigors of Planning

The research required to enter into a flight test program naturally separates into three spheres of concentration: (1) the **environment**, (2) the **mission**, and (3) the **system**.

Knowledge of all three is essential. Deficiencies in the understanding of any of the three significantly degrade the team's ability to construct and execute the test.

Know the Environment

Although the medium in which all air vehicles operate is the same (the earth's atmosphere), the conditions to which the air vehicle are exposed vary greatly. Forces of wind, humidity, temperature, and pressure combine to unforgiving extremes: violent heat and dryness in the desert climate (not to mention the effect of fine sand) to the frigid cold and thin air found at high altitudes.

Basic aviation and navigation face challenges in these two extremes, where air-breathing engines and lifting surfaces struggle to find sufficient mass to act upon, or heat and atmosphere combine to degrade

performance. Systems that find superior performance in controlled, limited test conditions can fail under the conditions found in the wild.

For example, sensor systems developed and tested in a controlled range with limited background noise and emissions may be optimized for performance in the wrong environment. When used in real-world conditions with a saturated electromagnetic environment, the processors that had no problem responding as designed yield unpredictable and sub-optimum performance.

Development of the Electromagnetic Surveillance Measures (ESM) system for the MH-60R helicopter was conducted on "quiet" ranges and inside of shielded hangars. The system was incredibly powerful and sensitive, capable of finding potential hostile or militarily significant emitters (i.e., radar systems employed by other military platforms).

However, the ESM system could only do this well when used over the open ocean or at low altitude and therefore shielded from a "noisy"

The **question** in flight test varies, depending on:

(1) Where the system is in development and acquisition
(2) Who is asking the question
(3) What decisions are to be made based on outcomes

environment. When taken into a coastal region or flown at a higher altitude, the system struggled to filter out the background radiation and "noise" from benign emitters with neutral, "non-interesting" purposes (e.g., coastal radars, commercial navigation).

The flight test professional must understand the intended operational environment and be aware of the differences found in the test environment. In particular, test design and subsequent interpretation of the results must factor in the impact of an environmental change.

Know the Mission

Without a thorough understanding of the ultimate purpose of the system (i.e., the *mission*), the tester may not be able to relate the test results to the end-user. Even when engaged in demonstration, discovery, or verification, the failure to consider the mission may result in misleading conclusions and recommendations.

During the early T&E of a system, often, the tester relies upon the requirements and capability descriptions being a correct interpretation of the essential performance required by the end-user to perform the desired task. But the test team must understand that the assumptions and conditions

when design engineers created the requirements change in the face of real-world events. The test team must be able to react to the changes and make crucial conclusions and recommendations based on the facts of the day.

The US Army's 1960s development of the Lockheed AH-56 Cheyenne aircraft is an example of *knowing the mission* and how it affects the test and the test environment. With a first flight in 1967, the Cheyenne was a dedicated ground-attack compound helicopter with a four-bladed rotor, a low-mounted wing, and a tail pusher propeller.[15]

The mission concept that drove the unique design relied on the aircraft's ability to enter a steep high-altitude dive over the battlefield. From this flight path, it would use the belly-mounted 30mm cannon to attack, with the tail propeller controlling airspeed in the descent and stabilizing the aircraft.

Although the aircraft's development faced many technical and programmatic issues (such as competition with the US Air Force for the Close Air Support mission), one change that led to its demise was on the battlefield. The enemy fielded a specialized radar-guided defense system particularly adept at locating and engaging high flying, slow-moving, diving aircraft.

Survivability and effectiveness of the Cheyenne's offensive capabilities were now in question—it could no longer perform the mission even if the technology worked as intended. One of the critical aspects of the AH-56 mission was operationally unsound, the program canceled, and the Army moved to a different concept.

The new direction led to the development of the AH-64 Apache, which entered service in the mid-1980s. The Apache operated in a radically different way—stay low, hide behind trees and terrain, and pop up to unleash a salvo of missiles, effectively neutralizing the capability of the radar-equipped defensive system.

Know the System
Perhaps an obvious requirement, but if the test team does not fully understand the system design, mainly its interaction with the environment and what functions it is to perform, a successful test is not likely.

One area where system knowledge is vital to test success is the modern flight control systems, which often seamlessly integrate navigation and aviation functions. It can be challenging to see where one ends, and the other starts.

For example, consider the sophisticated navigation system of the MH-60R. The system contained both Global Positioning System (GPS) and Inertial Navigation

Figure 9: Lockheed AH-56 Cheyenne

System (INS) technologies, combined into one component called an "Embedded GPS/INS," or EGI. During navigation system testing, the team explored the various initiation modes (ground, air, fixed, moving, cold/warm) of the two installed EGIs (#1 and #2).

The sophisticated technology and redundant design resulted in an extensive matrix of test conditions for the evaluation. The test team decided to break it up into individual test pieces and added them to other test events scheduled on the aircraft. This method is called **concurrent testing**. During each pre-flight brief, the navigation sub-system FTE would inform the aircrew about the combination desired for that day's flight.

On one particular day, the combination required a warm start of the #1 EGI before takeoff (thus, aligned before launch) and a post-launch cold start of the #2 EGI. The data collected was the time-to-align, as reported on the Navigation System Information display. The requirement for the EGI was to align under all conditions in less than 10 minutes. The crew intended to verify this for a #2 EGI in-air alignment, which could occur if power was interrupted for a sufficient amount of time while flying.

Soon after takeoff, the crew concentrated on setting up for a test of the radar system, the primary objective for that day. They flew straight and level, relying on the autopilot for *airspeed hold*

Figure 10: Lockheed Martin MH-60R Seahawk

at 120 knots. *Heading hold*, also an autopilot function, kept the aircraft on course, and the autopilot-controlled adjustment of engine power maintained altitude.

The crew was not thinking about the EGI test. Suddenly, the aircraft nose broke sharply right, uncommanded by the crew. They cycled off the autopilot and regained control of the aircraft, somewhat rattled by the abrupt and potentially dangerous maneuver they encountered.

Soon the crew realized what had happened: as required by the design spec, the aircraft Operational Flight Program (OFP) determined (incorrectly) that #2 EGI was aligned correctly, at precisely 9 minutes and 54 seconds after the in-air alignment was complete.

However, the #2 EGI did not agree with the #1 EGI about the helicopter heading. The autopilot was usually fed aircraft direction (for heading hold functionality) by the #2 EGI. But for the first 9.9 minutes of flight, it accepted the #1 EGI input and operating heading hold accordingly.

But for the first 9.9 minutes of flight, it accepted the #1 EGI input and operating heading hold accordingly.

When the #2 EGI was abruptly declared "good" by the OFP software, the flight control autopilot accepted the massive step-change in the heading value and responded as if the aircraft had encountered a sharp wind gust.

The test team did not correctly understand the interplay between a seemingly benign test (navigation functions and alignment) and a critical flight control function (autopilot).

The consequences were not tremendous (other than a scare to the pilots), but in another flight regime (hover, maximum power condition, landing), it could have been more problematic. The additional risk brought by combining tests for efficiency brought an unknown safety risk due to improper system knowledge.

Step 3. Make a Prediction

In Step 3, the scientist takes their understanding of the *Question* and their completed *Research* to construct a **hypothesis**. The hypothesis is about the phenomena they are studying. However, Step 3 is where the FTE, pursuing a flight test program, deviates from the scientist seeking new knowledge through the use of the traditional scientific method.

Instead of creating a hypothesis to explain an observation of something within the world, the FTE uses an understanding of the world and concepts and principles from disciplines such as physics, mechanics, aerodynamics, and electrical engineering to predict the response of the system to specific test environment and stimuli.

Thus *Step 3: Construct a Hypothesis* becomes *Step 3: Make a Prediction*.

Here it is important to understand requirements and design specifications. These are handy tools for a portion of the overall T&E effort. During *verification*, the tester seeks to measure system performance and compare the result directly to a pre-determined value or quality stated by the requirement. Then, the tester desires to make a factual statement regarding the relationship (using terms such as *met, pass, fail, exceed, below,* or *above*).

The requirements serve a vital purpose in the design of the system, as they are used to translate end-user needs into definitive, bounded, measurable, discrete, and (primarily) testable statements that guide the design engineer in their efforts.

Characteristics of a "Good" Requirement

- *Necessary* — *Need, vice a desire*
- *Feasible* — *Can be done*
- *Consistent* — *Not in conflict with other*
- *Affordable* — *Within budgetary contstraints*
- *Bounded* — *Not open-ended*
- *Correct* — *Accurately defined*
- *Singular* — *Not multi-part or compound*
- *Succinct* — *Concisely stated*
- *Complete* — *Contains all needed infomation*
- *And most of all: Testable!* — *Can be verified and validated!*

During verification, the FTE assesses how well the design matches the requirements. But test success does not equal passing requirements! The success of the test (or success of the test *prediction*) is not how it compares to the requirement, but instead how well it matches or reflects the actual system performance.

Thus the **prediction** is not merely whether or not the system passes the requirement. In the absence of other information, the underlying assumption is that the designer aimed to produce the response described by the requirement or specification.

But this is not necessarily always the case, for there are certainly performance parameters that the design intent was to exceed. Thus, the *hypothesis* or *prediction* should not be limited to the spec value but rather should be the actual anticipated system performance based on a good understanding of the environment, mission, and the system.

Generally, the team may approach DT&E with two assumptions, both of which serve as the starting **Prediction** until indicated otherwise. First, **the system has been built right**. The system should match the designer's intent, as expressed in the specification and requirements documents.

Second, **the right system has been built**. If the system provides the performance as required in the specification, then the end-user should be provided with the needed capability. Note that this assumes that the requirements are correct.

Requirements come from the *system engineering* process, which analyzes critical end-user requirements (including the KPPs described earlier) for meaning and intent to determine the performance necessary to meet expectations for the overall system (within technical, schedule, and cost constraints).

Once this **performance baseline** is defined, the various functions required to achieve the performance are also defined, creating the **functional baseline**. This description of the functions that the system must provide is further described by parsing the functions into tasks and sub-tasks.

The sub-tasks are then assigned to the various components and sub-systems in the overall system, thus making the **allocated baseline**. Finally, the allocated, functionally-aligned performance descriptions are decomposed into more numerous low-level (or greater detail, depending on perspective) spec requirements that guide the design.

The fidelity of the system engineering process, along with detailed accounting and tracing of the requirements back to the critical user needs, determines the quality of the overall requirements description. A high-quality requirements document, in turn, dictates whether or not the two fundamental assumptions are accurate: that *the system has been built right* and that *the right system has been built*.

Regardless of the design requirement quality or the designer's intent, the test team must make predictions regarding what the system does when tested. Also, the test team must determine what the mission requires the system to do (what it is *supposed* to do).

By doing this, every test on the system is tied back to one or both of two things: the requirement (verification) or the mission need (discovery, characterization, and validation).

The connection between the system performance and the mission need is the *mission relation* of the characteristic or performance parameter. The mission relation is the actual subject of each test during developmental test. Even during engineering tests, performed to measure performance values or to quantify a specific performance aspect, there is a tie back to the end-user, their needs, and the ultimate mission for the system.

Step 4a. Test: Write a Plan

Step 4, in the scientific method, fully expressed as "Test with an Experiment," further divides into two sub-steps. The first step, 4a, is to design a test that best answers the *Question* and then capture that design in a written test plan.

The test plan, if properly constructed, is a **critical thinking** tool used to walk the FTE through a logical sequence of thinking tasks, leading to a well-planned, safe, efficient, and practical test design,

which is a fundamental aim of every test program.

3 Reasons for a Written Test Plan

No one would start a journey to a destination with a required arrival time without any idea of what transportation to use, any plan for meals and accommodations, and without knowing the route.

Similarly, a test team does not start a test project without a plan. The test plan itself is not the objective of planning. Instead, it is the information obtained, decisions

Figure 11: Northrup Grumman E-2D Hawkeye

NAVAIR's Advanced Hawkeye Mission System Test Plan
has been active for over 5 years,
has involved over 120 people, and
has had over 70 amendments.

made, and thoughts generated during the process. At the end of test planning, regardless of the scope of the effort, the output is a written plan.

There are at least three purposes of a written test plan. The **first purpose** of the written test plan is to share knowledge throughout the members of the test team so that there is a common understanding of the test objectives, approach, and expected outcomes. In this way, the test plan represents a compiled thought process, ready to be shared with current and future test team members.

The future members are essential in this—they did not have the advantage of participating in the test planning process and did not hear the conversations that led to the test plan. However, they bring fresh eyes to the issues. The writer of the test plan must be sensitive to this, as "reading between the lines" cannot always be trusted to convey the proper meaning. What is plain and evident to someone close to the problems and issues may not be readily apparent to the fresh eyes.

Some tests are discrete events, lasting one or two flights. For these, future team members may not be of concern, because the test may be over before others have an opportunity to join.

But future test team members may include those assigned to assist documenting test results or may include future follow-on test efforts on the same or similar system. Thus the test plan documents the thought process intent for the reconstruction of what occurred and allows repeatability of the test and test conditions.

Other tests are long-term affairs, spanning months or years, with many team members coming and going, each with different needs. Those joining the team need to get up to speed quickly and understand the team's thoughts toward the test.

In contrast, those leaving may need a mechanism whereby they can document the things that they have seen and learned in the test process to ensure that their efforts are used rather than wasted. These are the first reasons why a test plan needs to be a dynamic, flexible document to accommodate different team members over some time.

Also, the test plan needs to be more than a static work because it must adapt and flex based on what the test team finds in the test. There may be changes to original assumptions as information becomes apparent, and differences in the expected versus actual risks before the team, often only fully understood after testing has commenced.

The **second purpose** of a written test plan is to enable oversight, but not burdensome, bureaucratic oversight that serves no useful purpose. In test design, oversight comes in the form of re-asking the question to make sure the team clearly understands it before heading in a misguided direction.

More importantly, oversight comes from senior testers who may have valuable lessons and best practices not formally documented, but only found in their memories. Often only by asking those who have *"been there"* and *"done that"* can flaws in test design be found and corrected before the test begins.

Testing often involves systems in a unique environment or with a new process in a technical area controlled from outside the test organization.

For example, the test planners must address airworthiness concerns and obtain the proper airspace use permissions. *Have we considered the hazards and potential consequences of our planned test and are sufficient risk controls in place? Are we going to be **safe**?*

Or perhaps the oversight is more of a management function, approving the use of personnel or resources for the test. *Do we have the right people and tools to work the problem, and are we **efficient**?*

As the test consumes high-value resources not owned by the team, oversight may come in the form of permission to proceed. Of particular concern is that the objectives of the test are correctly understood. *Is the proposed test going to answer the right questions and be **effective**?*

Oversight is an essential concept for flight test professionals. Flight test is inherently dangerous (with danger not only for the testers but also for others, both participants and non-participants). Test systems are expensive, and test methodology uses costly resources (prototypes, pre-production articles, instrumentation, range time, and support assets are costly, not to mention the expenses for labor).

Thus, it is often helpful for the test team to have pre-approval and agreement from those in positions of accountability before initiating a test effort. No flight test engineer would prefer to answer the questions that arise after the fact about test conduct and methodology (*What were you thinking? Who permitted you to do that?*), in addition to more complicated matters such as culpability and liability.

With any system of oversight, it is vital to separate the actions of the **doers** from the **approvers**. This separation means that those in a position requiring them to give oversight and grant permission should take care not to stray into a different role. They must avoid diving headlong into the test planning process and make decisions or trades for the test team. If they do, the result is that they no longer provide oversight as much as they approve of their efforts.

A principle within aviation maintenance is that a technician should never provide quality assurance or self-inspection of their work. The critical nature of the work they do requires two-person integrity. In aviation maintenance, the two-person integrity concept is sacred.

It is not very difficult to see how this concept would transfer to another aspect of aviation and guide the task of test planning. It is not enough for one person to plan and approve the test that they wrote. There must be a second set of eyes to survey and approve the test plan.

When an approver sees a plan that does not appear to be well thought out, with deficiencies in logic, with an improper procedure, or perhaps with incorrect assumptions, correction is appropriate. But correction and adjustment to the plan must be the test team's work and fully adopted and understood by them, not merely assent to the "whims" of the overseer.

Thus the review of a test plan is not merely an exercise of doing or writing whatever is required to "get it through review." Instead, it should be an opportunity to learn and improve. Since lives are on the line, it is a small price to pay to write, review, revise, and verify the test plan.

As a written document allowing for flight test oversight, the test plan becomes a contract between the team and leadership. After approval, the assumption can only be that the team adheres to the process, procedures, and methodology presented in the plan, not just in spirit but to the letter. The importance of the test plan is another essential flight test concept, paramount to safeguarding the integrity of the test and promoting **safety**, **efficiency**, and **effectiveness**.

The professional test team stops, evaluate, reassess, and coordinate with the approval authority before proceeding as changes arise during the test that lay outside of the test plan.

For example, conditions may change during the test from that expected (assumptions invalidated or adjusted). Or, unexpected results may drive the test away from the agreed-upon boundaries. The system performance leads to exciting but not approved areas of exploration.

When these sorts of things occur, the team revisits the planning process with a deliberate, concerted effort. They incorporate the new information into the planning process. They revise their test plan. Before returning to the test, the team obtains the authorization to proceed. The revision may add time and cost to the overall effort. Still, time and time again, the hazards are too significant, and the resources in play are too costly to approach with any other methodology.

Of course, the lower the stakes, risk, and expense, then more leeway is granted to the test team in the original test plan. Flexibility can be incorporated into the plan from the start, reducing the requirement for delays and rework of the plan.

Conversely, as the assessed risk probability and consequence increase, the rigor of the test planning process is appropriately increased to match, and the focus of the test plan narrowed.

Test Plan Purposes:

1. Share team knowledge

2. Enable leadership oversight

3. Direct test execution

Many test organizations categorize test efforts based on risk. They use the category to determine the proper approval level for the initial plan and subsequent changes. This workflow structure is paired with initial pre-test planning to identify who the team should consult with when planning. Knowledge of the reviewers and approvers before planning ensures that the team applies the appropriate depth of understanding and breadth of experience.

In this way, the organization does not leave the test team to their own devices in constructing (and defending) their plan grants the full range of resources available throughout the organization.

Following this model, once the test team has a developed, reviewed, and approved test plan, they are set free to execute the plan. They can do this on their own within the agreed-upon constraints of the plan, with the full assurance and backing of the larger organization behind them.

A second approach to test oversight brings the oversight closer to test execution than described above. In this model, the planning process is less focused on test methodology and objectives and more focused on the administrative and logistical concerns of the test effort. Once these issues are declared, solved, and documented via the test plan, leadership grants approval for the test plan only. Then the test conduct-related items (what to test, data collection priorities, test methods.) are brought together in test cards presented separately for review.

The team may proceed with their test after a review and signature on each of the test cards. However, the permission they received is limited to what they included on the specific test cards, submitted for that event.

FLIGHT TEST PROCEDURE CARD

SCALPEL EVALUATION

CARD # 15

	TARGET	TOLERANCES
DIVE ANGLE	0 degrees	
ALTITUDE	24,000 ft AGL	+/- 1000
MACH	0.75 IMN	+/- 0.02
AIRSPEED	450 KTAS	+/- 10

SCALPEL RELEASE PRACTICE RUN – GROUND LASE

- VERIFY LASER CODE 1688
- RANGE GIVES "**RANGE IS COLD**" CALL
- VERIFY RANGE RADAR ON
- SELECT **A/G** MASTER MODE
- MPCD SELECT/BOX **LGTR**
- SELECT **AUTO** DELIVERY MODE
- VERIFY STATION 3 SELECTED: **Q1, M1, N**
- ESTABLISH A RUN IN HEADING OF 325° TRUE
  - TGPT1 N **35° 51.665'** W **117° 40.094' EL. 2353**
- EXPECT "**CLEARED TO SIMULATE ARM AND RELEASE ON CONDITIONS**"
- **SIMULATE "LASER ON"**
- AT 5 SEC. PRIOR TO RELPT CALL "**SIMULATE CAMERAS ON**" AND "**STANDBY**"
- **SIMULATE** SPEED BRAKE SWITCH TO **RETRACT**
- OBTAIN RELEASE CONDITIONS
- **SIMULATE** MASTER ARM SWITCH TO **SAFE**
- **SIMULATE** SPEED BRAKE SWITCH TO **RETRACT**

DELIVERY PROFILE

450 KCAS / .75 IMN　　24,000' AGL →

Level Delivery / Recovery

Figure 12: Sample Flight Test Data Card

Even if the signed test plan covered other tests and scope, that part of the test is not available to the team until additional test cards are written and individually approved.

The second approach is not better or worse than the first. Each has strengths and weaknesses. A mix of the two may be appropriate based on the nature of the investigation. But they do reflect a different mindset toward oversight, an essential part of the flight test.

The **third purpose** of the test plan is to direct test conduct. As mentioned above, the data cards include step-by-step test procedures, reminders, and prompts (see example in Figure 12). Following the first ap-proach to oversight, the team devel-ops cards as an intermediate step be-tween the approved ready-to-execute test plan and the actual day and time of the event. Thus, the team must include all of the information neces-sary to develop robust, accurate, and helpful data cards in the initial test plan.

While data cards are highly personalized (they reflect the user's thought process) and tailored to make sense and are useful for the individual, some amount of standardization makes them valuable for the overall test and the entire team. A set of test cards often include unique cards specific to the roles of team members and standard cards useful for recording observed or measured data. Typically, the team creates cards for a specific test or subtest.

As such, test cards need to be readily identifiable and sortable by priority or sequence for the test event. They should prompt the requisite conditions for each test and provide essential reminders for safety and data accuracy concerns.

The test cards should allow adequate space when fill-in values are required, and also use a reasonable font size for ease of use. Finally, the cards should help orchestrate a thorough pre-event briefing, and a comprehensive post-event debrief and discussion.

The Test Plan

"In preparing for battle

I have always found that plans are useless,

but planning is indispensable."

— Dwight D. Eisenhower

The Test Plan

With the three reasons for a written test plan as a backdrop (provides a shared thought process, enables oversight and review, and orchestrates test execution), the test team focuses on three fundamental questions in constructing the test plan.

Part 1: What is the Question?

The first question that the test plan addresses is: *"What is the Question?"* Several sections of the test plan provide an answer to the reader. These three sections provide a clear understanding of the **subject** of the test, the **objective(s)** of the test, and the expected **outcome(s)** of the test.

Section 1: Background

The background provided in the test plan explains where the test effort lies in the overall life-cycle of the system, for example, whether the system is in the initial concept, design, prototyping, demonstration, development, verification, or validation process.

The background section answers several questions for the test team, including *"What has brought us to this point in the development?"* and *"Are we ready for the test?"*

In other words: *"Is the system on track for TRR or FRR completion and approval?* (See **Basics of Flight Test** for discussion of the two reviews.) Additionally, the background covers these questions:

1. Who is the audience for the test results? What decisions are made based on the results, conclusions, and recommendations the test team makes?

2. Are there agreed-upon test objectives to help determine the *effectiveness* and *suitability* of the system?

Test Plan Section 1: Background

- Short description of how and why behind the test, who requested, when needed, and who is performing
- Summary of previous test results, technical issues, reports, and technical literature that shapes or informs test risk management
- Summary of schedule and where this test fits into overall system development

---

3. What were the significant (relevant) findings from any previous testing on the system?

4. What developmental steps led to this test (e.g., changes to the design, corrections of past issues)?

The background section the table for the test and provides the necessary context for others to become active, involved, and informed members of the test team.

Section 2: Purpose

The next section of the test plan offers a concise statement of the purpose of the test program, test event, or test phase to be described in the test plan. The wording of the purpose is essential to convey the specific reason for the test.

The purpose must match the original tasking or question provided by either the sponsor of the test (the one who is paying for it). If there is no external sponsor, then it must come from the team itself as they work with designers to develop the system under test. Words that have definite connotations include:

Measure

Use engineering methods to determine a value, level, or characterization of performance or quality of the system. Typically obtaining the value is the aim of the test for another organization (apart from test team) to analyze and evaluate.

Test

Subject the system to a defined set of conditions and determine the response. As with measurement, a

---

Test Plan Section 2: Purpose

Test Objectives
- Briefly state specific test objectives (e.g., demonstrating specific performance capabilities; compliance with regulatory/statutory certification requirements; validation of operational suitability, effectiveness, and mission profiles; or verification of corrections)

Success Criteria
- Identify what is required to successfully complete the test (i.e., minimum adequate testing and data re-quired)
- Identify applicable specifications or requirements against which system performance is evaluated

---

test in itself does not imply analysis, comparison, or judgment of the merits of the values obtained.

Determine
Same as measure or test.

Evaluate
Go beyond measurement and test by assessing the merits of the system, given a specific understanding of the intended environment, expected mission, anticipated end-user, and tactics/procedures for operational use. Evaluation typically requires an estimation of what the end-user expects from the system to meet basic capability needs.

Verify
To compare the measured or tested values against the specification requirements to determine if the system failed to meet, met, or exceeded the requirements. Verification is not an evaluation; instead, it is a statement of fact.

Validate
Same as evaluate.

Quantitative
Numerically based data, information, assessment, verification, or validation.

Qualitative
Non-numerically based test. Not necessarily subjective, as there are qualitative characteristics that present as binary conditions or discrete states. If subjective, the FTE must take care to construct objective test criteria and methods.

Additionally, the purpose section should introduce the applicable specs and requirements documents for the performance comparison of the system. Understanding of the evaluation standards helps to explain the test **success criteria**, whether it is gathering sufficient information for verification or supporting an evaluation. The purpose should include the minimum testing to complete and the minimum data to collect.

Section 3: Description
The final piece required to adequately explain to the reader the question behind the test program is a description of the system under test. As intended, the description section is not a complete, detailed blow-by-blow covering the design intricacies. Instead, it is a highly focused, tailored discussion accurately informing the reader of what they need to know to participate in the test.

The level of detail in the description section depends on the system under test. If the test is an evaluation for effectiveness and suitability for a particular mission or task, then the description should describe that mission or task.

If the test is to verify spec compliance, then the essential components or sub-systems assigned to give the desired performance should be described. The intent is not to make the reader a design expert.

At a minimum, the description should provide a clear understanding of two things: (1) where and how the data are to be collected from the system and (2) what features of the system are of particular concern (for safety, performance, or testing).

For example, if testing involves the integration of new communications hardware into an existing air vehicle, the description should focus on the location of the component within the air vehicle.

Additionally, the description should include the interfaces the component needs (power, data, cooling) and any changes to the original air vehicle required to accommodate it. Finally, the description should explain the mission areas, tasks, functions, or

---

Test Plan Section 3: Description

System Under Test
- Physical description, focusing on relevant attributes.
- Highlight upgrades or changes (hardware, software, system operation)
- Modifications made to support the test (e.g., tethers, flight termination system)
- State whether the system is production representative

Instrumentation
- Internal instrumentation (accelerometers, strain gauges, pressure transducers)
- External (radar, weather balloons, photo, video, audio)
  Note: Consider using a table to show parameter, source, description, sample and update rates, accuracies

Concept of Operations
- Briefly describe the employment concept: intended users, intended use (mission); operational environment
- Briefly describe the sustainment concept: maintenance and logistics support plans, reliability/availability goals

---

capabilities that interface with the new system or component.

In this example, the description then explains the design of the new component, the operational concepts, and any changes or modifications required to support the test. The description's level of detail corresponds to the level of test, insight required, and the component's significance toward airworthiness, safety, and mission success of the overall system (i.e., if instrumental for safety, then more details may be needed to test safely). See the previous description of *white box, black box,* and *gray box* in **Levels of Flight Test**.

The description should detail the required test instrumentation, including gear installed in (or on) the air vehicle and external instrumentation from chase aircraft, ground facilities, range assets. The description of the data sources should include required accuracy, data rates, sources of error, and other details for the successful collection of necessary data. A table is a great way to present test instrumentation.

Another aspect of instrumentation is the **category** by impact to test safety, effectiveness, and efficiency. The test plan repeatedly refers to categories, such as when discussing safety and test method. The instrumentation categories and definitions are:

Safety of Flight (SOF)

Parameter or data must be available and referenced during all aspects of flight to provide adequate safety. Examples include airspeed, altitude, engine temperature, fuel quantity. In other words, any parameter that would ultimately be made available to the end-user during routine operations would be considered SOF.

Additionally, during the development of a new system, there are often parameters that may not make it to the final cockpit/control station instrumentation readout but are necessary to gain understanding and confidence in system operation.

Safety of Test (SOT)

This parameter or data must be available and referenced during specific test events or maneuvers to provide safety. Often these parameters are identified while constructing risk mitigations during the Test Hazard Analysis (THA) process.

If a SOT parameter is not available or working during a test flight that

> **Safety of Flight (SOF)**
> need for flight safety
>
> **Safety of Test (SOT)**
> need for test safety
>
> **Analysis Critical (AC)**
> need for test success

requires it, then the test must be halted, and the problem corrected before that test resumes. An example SOT parameter might be the real-time output of a vibration transducer displayed in the control room during flutter testing (or envelope expansion).

Analysis Critical (AC)

This parameter or data must be available for the successful completion of the test. Depending on the test methodology, the parameter may or may not require real-time monitoring to execute the test. Either way, the data must be recorded in some fashion for post-event processing to generate the appropriate test results and answer the test question.

Unless previously covered while describing the air vehicle or system, the test plan should include the **Concept of Employment** (CONEMP): *How are you going to use it?* Or, if more appropriate, the description includes a **Concept of Operations** (CONOPS): *How will the system fit into the overall mission, potentially in concert with other systems currently fielded or intended?*

Including both the CONEMP and the CONOPS in the test plan could lead to a lengthy discussion. Referencing previously-published (and readily available) documents

is an acceptable way to prevent this and keep the test plan focused. However, if this section of the test plan gets too lengthy, a best practice is to use an appendix. This approach applies to any section of the test plan. Pull material that would distract the reader from the main story (even if it is necessary) out and put it in an appendix.

There is a great way to provide structure and order to the test plan. With all of the various systems, components, functions, and missions that need to be in the description section, it can become a rambling, confusing mess. Therefore, think of the test plan like a filing cabinet with various drawers or "bins" for the different information.

A goal when writing a test plan is to not repeat information unnecessarily, as the inherent risk to repetition is forgetting to update all references when the information changes, therefore making the plan inconsistent. The filing cabinet approach helps to prevent that. After identification, each piece of information naturally gravitates to the correct location in the test plan format.

For the description section of the test plan, the next page contains a suggested logical structure for presenting needed information to the reader:

1) Description of the basic Air Vehicle, with particular attention to the essential knowledge needed to conduct a test of the system

2) Any changes to basic Air Vehicle to support test, and what impact to results

3) A description of the system under test, with details including operations, expected environment, performance predictions, safety concerns, and past issues

4) Any changes made to the system under test, with any impact to results

5) Description of installed instrumentation in air vehicle or system under test

6) Description of other instrumentation (external to air vehicle), ground support facilities, ranges, and chase aircraft

7) List of parameters with data rate, collection method, range, frequency, error, and instrumentation category (SOF, SOT, AC)

8) CONEMP or CONOPS: identify end-user; intended mission, task, or function; and operational environment

9) Sustainment concept: maintenance and logistics support planning, sustainment goals (e.g., inherent reliability, availability, and mean time between failure)

Part 2: How to Answer the Question?

The test plan first provides the reader with an in-depth understanding of the question at the center of the test program. Next, the test plan describes how that question is to be answered by the test. Proper attention to this part of the planning process prevents the team from finishing the test with a pile of data but no idea what to do with it.

Additionally, the effort put into proper planning helps prioritize and ensure that the most important data are collected even when faced with reduced time and money.

Section 4: Scope

The scope section outlines the extent of the test program, with different dimensions to describe test details such as when and where, the number of flights, and estimated ground and flight hours. Also, scope identifies the test start and finish dates and any fixed schedule constraints, such as scheduled use of external resources and infrastructure. The scope is the first indication for the reader of the size and magnitude of the test effort.

Next, the scope section describes the test envelope by detailing the conditions the system encounters in the proposed test. The conditions include descriptions of how high, how far, how fast, under what forces, and with what loading. This envelope is compared to the existing system limits (either from the airworthiness clearance, designer limitations, or other operational limitations) using a text description, a table, or a figure.

If the test envelope projects outside standard operating conditions, the reader expects details of how these test points are collected safely. The writer addresses details of the procedure to do this in the method section (right after scope).

Some data points are **static** in that the conditions can be approached slowly with caution. Other points are **dynamic** in that there are maneuvers required to place the system in that position in the test envelope. If dynamic data points are near the test envelope or flight restriction boundaries, the reader expects to read how to approach these points without overshoot or restriction violation.

Regarding flight restrictions, the scope section must fully identify them. Also, the test plan includes unique restrictions placed on the system under test due to instrumentation installation, test range restrictions, or other sources (such as testing an immature system without all of the planned capability).

A test plan appendix typically contains any specific documents about the use of the system (e.g., fight clearance(s), airworthiness certification, system release paperwork).

After giving the test scope, test envelope, and test restrictions, the test plan provides a list of tests. The list gives the specific conditions (found within the test envelope) and details the test condition tolerances.

Called the **Test & Test Conditions (T&TC)** table (often referred to as the **Test Matrix**), it is used later in the construction of the test data cards.

The T&TC table lists warm-up, practice, or build-up points. An explanation of the purpose of these points shows the team's understanding of their importance. If some are optional, then they need to be indicated as such; otherwise, they are mandatory.

Test Plan Section 4: Scope

Overall
- Summary of the program, including when and where the test will be executed, number of flights, ground and flight hours, calendar days
- Identify test start/finish dates and schedule con-straints

Test envelope
- Test environment (how high, far, and fast; forces; loads)
- Compare the test envelope to the system limits using description, table, or figure

Flight authorizations/restrictions
- Discuss airworthiness certifications, RF spectrum ap-proval, FAA/FCC certifications, airspace authorizations
- Restrictions (e.g., dry due to instrumentation)

Tests and Test Conditions (T&TC)
- Table of specific test points, test conditions (with tolerances), and data collected
- If applicable: configuration, loading, buildup, pre-requisite points or training, remarks, and risk category (in appendix if more than one page)

Build-up

The plan requires the completion of a build-up test point before proceeding to the next point. The need for build-up points may vary, including:

1) **Safety concerns** with the final data point require starting with benign conditions before pushing to the edge of the envelope for the ultimate objective.
2) The **data collection** technique is complicated, such that exercising the data and instrumentation process before attempting the desired data point.
3) Concern for the safety of the air vehicle or system requires **real-time monitoring** of parameter(s). As the test moves toward increasingly

severe maneuvers, the decision to continue is made based on the parameter(s).

Warm-up/Practice

The data point may be repeated by the operator as needed to ensure that they can achieve the target conditions. The team inserts practice data points into the plan when the conditions are challenging to achieve, or the tolerance is small. Data collection during warm-up and practice points is optional.

Warm-up or practice points are training events built into the test plan, especially when the configuration or loading of the air vehicle is new, and there is no other way for the operator to gain experience with it other than during the test.

Test Plan Section 4: Scope (continued)

Configurations/loadings
- Table(s) of software loads, aircraft aerodynamic configurations (gear, flaps, slats, bay doors, wing sweep), and loadings (payload, fuel, center of gravity, gross weight)
- Label configurations being tested with discrete identifiers (i.e., A/B/C or 1/2/3)

Limitations to scope
- Envelope constraints, modes, or configurations not tested; reason (e.g., cost, schedule, equipment, personnel); and impact on overall evaluation
- Non production representative elements of system
- Differences between test and operating envelope

Prerequisite

The test plan calls out the collection of some data points in a specific order to allow for analysis and decision making. Often these are appropriate for envelope expansion tests (*discovery* or *characterization*). Further descriptions may be needed to direct if the team must obtain the prerequisite point during the same test event and conditions, or if collection during a previous test flight suffices.

Regarding configurations and loadings, the scope section describes them in a table or figure. Configurations include hardware/software versions and position of moveable aerodynamic components (e.g., gear, flaps, slats, bay doors, wing sweep). Test loading includes items such as payload details, fuel amount, location of the center of gravity, gross weight, and stores.

Discrete identifiers label the various configurations and loadings. Then the T&TC table uses those identifiers to describe the required test point conditions. Typically configurations are referred to by an acronym, letter, or number and loadings by a different set of identifiers to help the test team keep them separate.

Finally, the test plan includes any limitations to the scope of the test, such as envelope constraints (areas to avoid), operating modes,

or configurations not evaluated. For each limitation, the test plan should outline the reason (e.g., cost, schedule, equipment, personnel) and the overall impact on the evaluation.

The limitations to scope may also include a discussion of elements of the system that are not production representative and the differences between the test envelope and operating envelope.

Section 5: Method

After describing the dimensions of the test in the scope section, the test plan method details the step-by-step process to obtain each test condition. Also, the method includes data collection and data analysis descriptions, which completes the picture of how the team intends to answer the test question(s).

Method begins with a discussion of specific preparations required, including qualifications and training for test team members and support personnel. There may be non-standard pre-test procedures for the system, instrumentation, or test equipment (system weighing, support equipment calibration), which each need planning and budgeting.

Before each test event, a pre-test brief ensures that the team is ready to execute. The method section includes briefing details, such as what guide(s) to use, who attends, and the contents of the brief. More discussion of the pre-test brief is found below in **Test Execution**.

Also covered in the pre-test brief, and detailed in the method section of the test plan, are test-specific *go/no-go criteria*. These are pre-planned factors or conditions with the accompanying action to take if the unable to meet the condition. *Go/no-go* criteria are for areas of concern such as weather, system issues, instrumentation, range or airspace clearance, flight termination system, communication systems, or telemetry status.

Often the most transparent way to communicate *go/no-go* criteria is a table which shows "**If...**" (condition) "**Then...**" (action). Typical actions include **Cancel**, **Delay**, **Hold**, **Go**, and **No-go**. A best practice is to include a revisit time or duration for any Delay or Hold status.

Central to the method section of the test plan are step-by-step procedures, techniques, and methods for each test described in the scope section. If available, the method section references standard procedures already defined in documentation or manuals. Build-up, warm-up, and practice are described, along with a plan for progression from one point to the next (particularity in envelope expansion tests).

There may be operational countdowns, switchology, and unique or critical terminology for the test. *Switchology* is a made-up word that describes the flow, sense, and use of the multitude of switches, buttons, levers, and controls in the cockpit or on the ground station to perform the desired aviation, navigation, and communication functions. Operators often need a straightforward set of instructions describing what to do and when. If appropriate, the method can include a flow chart for sequence or decision.

However, a flight test isn't as simple as getting to a specified flight condition; it also includes collecting data and using that data to answer the question.

The method section continues with a discussion of data collection: what data each test requires, how data are collected (bus data, telemetry, hand-held data cards, and surveys), and who is collecting it. Since this ties in directly to the T&TC table presented in the scope section and the instrumentation table in the description section, it may make sense to refer to those tables and add additional columns as required.

Test Plan Section 5: Method

Test preparation

- Identify pretest training and qualifications requirements test participants (e.g., support personnel, test engineers, operators)
- Discuss non-standard pre-test procedures for the system, instrumentation, or test equipment (e.g., weighing, calibration)

Pre-test brief

- State who is required to be at pre-test brief
- Describe the specific briefing guide(s) to be used, including:

  1) Test objectives
  2) Configuration/loading
  3) Test points, methods
  4) *Knock it off criteria*
  5) Limitations/restrictions
  6) Backup test points/alternate
  7) Special precautions
  8) THAs, emergencies
  9) Review of *go/no-go* criteria
  10) No-vote philosophy

Test-specific *go/no-go* criteria

- Factors/conditions required and action if not met (e.g., weather, system requirements, instrumentation, range/airspace clearance, flight termination system; comms/ telemetry status)

Detailed Method of Test (DMOT)

- State how each test will be conducted: test techniques, procedures, and maneuvers
- Reference standard procedures already defined in documentation or manuals
- Identify prerequisites and build-up for point progression or envelope clearance
- Include operational countdowns, switchology, and unique/critical terminology
- If appropriate, flow chart for test sequence or decision pro-cess

Data collection

- Identify what data is required for each test, how/who will be collect (bus data, telemetry, hand-held data cards, surveys)
- Specify instrumentation category (SOF, SOT, AC)

Test Plan Section 5: Method (continued)

Real-time data monitoring
- dentify data parameters for real-time monitoring (by whom)
- Describe techniques to detect and stop adverse trends: what actions will be taken, when they will be taken, and by whom
- Describe process to clear progression to next test point

Debrief
- Identify personnel required at post-test debrief
- Debrief should include:

  1) Safety issues   4) Deficiencies (and who will document)

  2) Admin issues   5) Lessons Learned

  3) Review of data   6) Action(s) required prior to next test

Data analysis
- Discuss tools, methods, models, simulations, statistical techniques, and accuracy requirements for reduction and analysis

---

Safety of Flight or Safety of Test (SOF/SOT) parameters may require real-time data monitoring. The goal of monitoring is to detect and stop adverse trends; thus, the plan must identify the actions to be taken, when to take them, and who takes them. When encountering adverse conditions, there should be a documented process directing the decision to proceed to the next test point and to resume the test.

As with the pre-test brief, a post-event debrief is necessary to complete the test event. The method section includes details regarding the brief, which is discussed later in **Test Execution**.

Finally, the method section needs to connect data, information, results, and answers. Unique data reduction and analysis tools, methods, models, simulations, statistical techniques, and accuracy requirements are all valid discussion topics to give the reader a complete understanding of the plan and approach.

Part 3: What Could Go Wrong?

First, the test plan gives the *Question* (background, purpose, and description), then how to answer it (scope and method). Now, the last part of the Tet Plan answers the question: *"What could go wrong?"*

The scope and method sections, devised to answer the test question, are the primary recipients of this fundamental inquiry. Presumably, the scope and method are **safe**, **efficient**, and **effective**. Now is the opportunity to prove it.

The proof is given in the last two sections: risk management (contributes to **safety**), and project management (contributes to **efficiency** and **effectiveness**).

Section 6: Risk Management

The test risk management approach uses system safety tools to identify, mitigate, and categorize residual risk for test-specific hazards. The heart of this process is the **Test Hazard Analysis (THA)** approach, which is detailed later, immediately following the discussion of the test plan.

In the risk management section, a summary of the THA findings are presented in a table format and included in an appendix, suitable for use in the pre-test briefing to remind the test team of the hazards and planned mitigation steps. The most severe THA found during the assessment is the basis for the overall hazard/risk level of the test.

Then, a **Safety Checklist (SC)**, used as a thinking tool, ensures thorough coverage of test issues gained by the test team and organization throughout their experiences in flight test with the current or past systems.

The SC is essentially a list of institutional lessons learned from past flight tests. Many represent mistakes, accidents, and near-accidents. The SC does not indicate what to do about the issues it contains. Instead, it serves as a reminder to the test team to address areas of concern, both general and specific.

Test Hazard Analysis
process to identify, mitigate, and monitor test-specific hazards

Safety Checklist
guide to help ensure the planning process covers issues of concern

---

For example, a typical SC entry may ask whether the test involves the use of a laser or requires laser emissions. The SC would prompt the test team to consider the potential hazards and implications of laser use and answer the SC question with the reference of where in the test plan are the detail regarding laser use.

As the team works through the checklist, each item response is "No," "N/A," or "Yes." With a "Yes" answer, the writer gives the internal test plan paragraph or page reference.

If the test organization develops an extensive SC listing (NAVAIR's is over 60 items), other rules simplifying its use may be appropriate (such as skipping sections that don't apply). Test plan writers should avoid deleting individual questions to prevent confusion for those expecting the standard (customary) listing.

The completed SC acts as a guide to where the test plan addresses routine or recurring safety issues. The SC is particularly useful for a sizeable DT&E organization such as NAVAIR, with many test plans written and executed simultaneously across many disciplines and areas. The concept is compelling and effective in preventing issue recurrence through awareness and visibility.

Section 7: Project Management
The test does not run itself. Even if all of the safety concerns are identified and mitigated, many other issues exist that threaten successful completion, including:

Test Plan Section 6: Risk Management

Test Hazard Analysis
- Identify overall test risk category
- Reference the THA appendix
- Present a table of hazards and residual risk levels

Safety Checklist
- Reference the safety checklist appendix
- Identify remarkable aspects of the safety checklist

Additional special precautions
- Discuss any additional precautions or risk controls
- Describe modifications or additions to normal or emergency procedures

---

(1) Not having the right people, in the right place, at the right time

(2) Premature consumption of test team resources (calendar time, travel money, labor hours, fuel)

(3) Misalignment of contracts for test articles with the test program schedule

(4) Improper coordination of facilities, infrastructure, or support the team is borrowing, renting, or leasing

The project management section begins by detailing the test plan oversight process. The plan identifies the reviewers and approvers of the test plan and subsequent amendments or

---

Test Plan Section 7: Project Management

Test plan administration
- Identify test plan reviewers and approvers
- Discuss test plan approval and change procedures

Funding/schedule
- Identify funds allotted, their source, and expiration
- Identify major test milestones (first test, test plan need date, test beginning and end, test phases, reports)

Personnel requirements
- Identify personnel assigned to the project (test engineers, operators, test conductor, photographers) with contact info

Facilities/support requirements
- Discuss facilities and test ranges which require special scheduling or coordination
- Define timeline for scheduling, coordination briefs, site surveys, advance pack-up and shipping
- Identify points of contact
- Describe other resources and timeframe (e.g., support aircraft, targets, weapons/stores/expendables, ground support equipment, laboratories, data services, photo and shop support)

Reports
- Discuss types of reports, distribution, and timing

revisions. If the sponsor of the test plan is an outside agency (i.e., test for hire), these reviewers and approvers need to know how much time they need to commit to the task.

Following a discussion of who is involved in oversight, the next topic is the funding and schedule resources allocated to the test effort. The test plan should include any resource-imposed constraints on test execution (e.g., no earlier than or no later than dates).

A test schedule in the plan lists major test milestones. The schedule can be a simple description or figure showing test events, progression, and critical path for the program.

Personnel requirements, detailed in the test plan, provide the names of the people either on the test team or supporting the test, their unique skill sets and qualifications, contact information, and other data (currency and training information).

The listing of the people involved in the test is followed by a similar description of the facilities and support infrastructure, including scheduling information, point(s) of contact, and logistics/coordination details.

Finally, the project management section ends with a description of the documentation plan for the test effort. No test is complete without a report, and the test plan must make the reader, approver, and test participant aware of the expectations and responsibilities for reporting.

The Complete Test Plan

After describing the body section of the test plan, and before returning to the comparison of the flight test discipline with the scientific method, it is essential to pause and take a look at the complete test plan.

A well-constructed test plan contains more than the seven named sections encompassing the body. Other components are equally crucial for managing the information in the test plan, ensuring that the information gets to the right people, and packaging the information in an accessible, understandable way.

Cover Sheet
The test plan cover sheet is essential in identifying four items:

(1) Whatthe project is (title)
(2) When the project is (dates)
(3) Who is executing the test project (names)
(4) Who is involved in the review and approval (oversight)

The reader of the test plan can easily find this information outright from the front cover, and those involved in the writing, review, and approval of the plan have no doubt where it is in the process.

If the organization chooses to administer the test planning process in a completely electronic format, the use of digital signatures (or some similar means) gives process insight. Still, there must be definitive action required by the reviewers and approvers, for only after the final signature does the team know that the plan they have written is backed and supported by the organization.

Signature Page
Inside the front cover of a paper test plan, the test team signature page should contain the assent from the members of the team who participate in the test. By signing, the team members are acknowledging three key points:

(1) They have **read** the entire test plan with updates or changes.
(2) They **understand** their role in the test plan and have addressed questions or concerns.
(3) They are **ready** and **able** to carry out their part in the plan.

This signature page should be redone after any test plan update or revision to ensure that all involved in the test have the most up-to-date information.

Although it sounds onerous, only strict adherence to the test plan signature and assent process (for reviewers, approvers, and test team members) ensures that the plan has a chance to be followed. Without it, test execution is in jeopardy, for it only takes one test team member who doesn't understand or know their job to lead to disaster.

Table of Contents (TOC)

The TOC helps the reader find the information they need. A small test, with a small plan, may not require a TOC. Although some references provide a page number beyond which a TOC is mandatory, perhaps a better guide would be whether or not there are any Appendices which would require the reader to maneuver through the document in other than a linear manner.

Test Plan Contents

- Cover Sheet
- Signature Page
- Table of Contents (optional)
- Change/Revision Log
- Software Version Log (if applicable)
- Test Plan Body
    1. Background   5. Method
    2. Purpose   6. Risk Management
    3. Description   7. Project Management
    4. Scope
- References
- Acronyms and Abbreviations
- Appendices (typical)
    1. Detailed Description(s), such as:
        A. Flight Control Description (FCD)
        B. Mission System Description (MSD)
        C. Concept of Operations (CONOPS)
        D. Concept of Employment (CONEMP)
    2. Flight Clearance (FC) or Airworthiness
    3. Instrumentation List
    4. Test and Test Conditions (T&TC)
    5. Operational Countdown
    6. Detailed Method of Test (DMOT)
    7. Test Hazard Analysis (THA)
    8. Safety Checklist (SC)

Change Log(s)

Following the TOC, two different changelogs are appropriate. The **first changelog** is for the test plan itself to give a quick and easy-to-follow history of the dynamic planning document. Any test team member can quickly find out what pages a change affected.

The changelog should help the reader. Thus, it should include the date of the change, a reference number, affected page(s), and a short description of the change.

A test plan change affects only a few pages in the document, whereas a revision affects the entire document or major sections. Again, to help the reader, the reference number in the changelog could refer to changes (e.g., CH 1) by a number and revisions by a letter (e.g., REV A).

The **second changelog** is optional, depending on the nature of the configuration management and the airworthiness process requirements for the system and air vehicle under test.

If allowed, the **software version log** tracks the dates of each revision to the loaded software used in the test, to keep the test moving (*efficient*) while being mindful of the importance of tracking what configuration is under test at what time (*effective*).

For matters of **safety**, where the software influences the control of the air vehicle, the use of a software version log is not often viable. The airworthiness process requires flight clearance (or other documentation) updates and re-release for each software change.

Test Plan Body

After the changelog(s), the test plan includes the body of the plan, which has the seven sections described above, that serve to answer the vital test planning questions of:

(1) What is the question?
(2) How will the question be answered?
(3) What could go wrong?

References

Behind the body, the references are listed in the order that they appear in the body. Typical references include published background information (project overview), system descriptions or operation documents (user's manuals, operator's guides), standard test methods (handbooks, manuals), and previous test reports.

The determining factors for whether or not to use a reference are:

(1) **Availability**
Obscure or controlled distribution documents may not be appropriate).

(2) **Quantity**

If there are only a few words, sentences, or paragraphs, an appendix may be easier for the reader.

(3) **Stability**

If the reference is subject to recurring review and update, an appendix or enclosure may be better to make sure the reader has the same version.

If the test plan references documents consulted during planning, the page or paragraph identifying the specific location in the reference is preferred. No reader appreciates open-ended references to a large manual without knowing what to look for or where to look.

Acronyms and Abbreviations

Any acronyms or abbreviations used in the test plan should be listed alphabetically in a table. Often a tedious task for the writer to collect and collate, a well-written list is essential to ensure proper understanding of the plan's technical content.

Perhaps the test team develops a standard list of acronyms appropriate for the entire effort and does not need a separate list in each test plan. Still, in that case, it should be clear to the reader where they can get information. Standard practice is to write out an abbreviation the first time before using it. However, the writer should always feel free to spell out the entire meaning anytime to reduce confusion and increase understanding.

Appendicies

Finally, the back of the test plan should include various appendices. Some are standard; some are optional. The basic rule of thumb is to use an appendix anytime the material gets so bulky that leaving it in the body section would interrupt the flow of understanding for the reader. Additionally, if the data is secondary or highly detailed such

---

Test Reports

Regarding the task of test reporting:

At this point (before executing the test) the team has written a large amount of information about the test in the Test Plan. Much of this will be reused, which gives the test team a head start on the final report and documentation!

In fact, the more effort spent early in thinking about how the final report will address and answer the question, the simpler that job will be.

---

that separate consideration would help, it should be in an appendix.

Once the information is in an appendix, it is much easier to swap it out during a test plan revision or pull it out separately for reference during test execution.

Typical test plan appendices include:

Flight Control Description (FCD)
A detailed discussion of the air vehicle control system, tracing control axes, motion paths, or channels.

Mission System Description (MSD)
A technical discussion of one or more of the sensor systems on the air vehicle. The MSD usually includes software and hardware, signal paths, and command/control relationships.

Concept of Operations (CONOPS)
A discussion that focuses on the user and how they would operate the system to accomplish their objective. The CONOPS often combines environments, missions, and tactics into a hybrid scenario or profile.

Concept of Employment (CONEMP)
A high-level description of how to use the system on a day-to-day basis vice a specific sortie or mission profile. The CONEMP often shows relationships with other systems, interoperability issues, and interfaces.

Flight Clearance (FC)
Authorization required for flight in the configuration required for test (see the **Three-Legged Stool of Flight Test**), with particular regard to any limitations or restrictions imposed by the authorization and how the planned test avoids a violation.

Instrumentation List
Details of all internal and external data sources with particular regard to data rate, frequency, range, accuracy, recording method, and parameter category (SOF, SOT, AC).

Test and Test Conditions (T&TC)
Essential to all tests, this table records the test name, targeted conditions and tolerances, test variables, priority, test phases, residual risk (from THA), and an indication of the method (by name or title).

Operational Countdown
Step by step listing of actions required to get to the test, typically given days, hours, and minutes to go for each step with person or role responsible for each.

Detailed Method of Test (DMOT)
Typically called DMOT only when a separate appendix otherwise contained in the method

section, provides procedures and descriptions of non-standard or unique test set-up and execution.

Test Hazard Analysis (THA)

A table of the THA items providing hazard identification, mitigation, and residual risk categorization. Test phases, test names, or test events provide a natural segregation of the THAs so that each THA is assigned only to the applicable specific tests where the hazard resides.

Safety Checklist (SC)

Essentially a topical cross-reference index to the test plan, demonstrating that the test planning process was of adequate breadth to cover all appropriate areas of concern. The organizational testing culture and experience (lessons learned) determined the areas included in the current SC guidance.

The completed test plan provides a one-stop-shopping approach to all the information required for the test team member to become a fully functioning participant in the test: that should be the writer's ultimate goal.

A signed test plan is approved and ready to execute by a flight test professional with the appropriate *know-ledge*, *ability*, and *skill* (KAS) background. No additional approvals or authority is required, except for the scheduling of test assets and resources.

> A **signed** Test Plan is
>
> *Approved* and
>
> *Ready-to-Execute*

Test Risk Management

"A superior test pilot is one who uses

his superior intellect to avoid situations

that will require the use of his superior skill."

— Author unknown
Quote found on the walls
of the US Naval Test Pilot School

Test Risk Management

Managing risk is nothing new—the essentials of leadership, critical thinking, and the acquisition disciplines of program management, system engineering, and logistics all require risk-based decision making, which in turn requires a deliberate risk management approach.

Aviation requires continual cooperation with a robust risk management system. For human beings defying the law of gravity is not natural and, therefore, inherently dangerous.

Every aviation organization uses a risk management program to reduce their exposure to the hazards of flight. Their success in minimizing accidents is proportional to the emphasis and resources dedicated to the process. However, it is tough to credit "saves" directly to the risk management system.

The approach used by the Test Team should augment and not supplant established, functioning risk management systems in use by professional aviators and UAS operators.

Thus the focus of the Test Risk Management effort should center squarely on the additional risk assumed due to the execution of the test plan's method within the scope.

This aim has given rise to a risk management methodology used for the NAVAIR flight test process, called *Test Hazard Analysis (THA)*. The process involves collaborative test risk identification, mitigation, and control steps designed to reduce test risk to acceptable residual risk levels. Additionally, THA categorizes individual tests and the overall test programs to enable a two-tiered risk handing philosophy: mitigation through organizational test execution procedures and mitigation through individual test team processes.

Risk

Expression of loss in terms of likelihood of occurrence and the severity of the impact

The Importance of Flight Test Discipline

Otto Lilienthal was one of the world's first test pilots, but he was also what we call today a flight test engineer. Both roles are critical to efficient and effective test design and safe execution.

A story from the early days of naval aviation flight test, told by one of its most experienced flight test engineers, serves to emphasize this point. The flight test engineer's father was an original pioneer of the flight test discipline back in the 1950s.

> "I clearly remember one day when I was 6 that my father was late coming home for dinner. My mother and I were at the dinner table eating when he finally arrived home, and without a word, sat down at the table, quietly shifting his food around his plate and not speaking or eating.
>
> "My mother finally said, 'Honey, what's wrong; you're not eating,' and with a tear in his eye, my father looked up and said, 'I killed someone to-day.'
>
> "And that was my introduction at a young age to the world of flight test, and I will never forget it."

Today, with the advent of better safety systems, test discipline has been driven into the foundations of the flight test process. However, we quickly forget the extreme and frequent sacrifices made in the early days of flight test. That is what should scare every modern flight test engineer and test pilot.

The more time that spans between flight test mishaps means that the discipline can quickly wane in the name of program expediency. And yet once that fateful day occurs, all fingers will point at the flight test team and their "flawed test design."

Test Hazard Analysis (THA)

The first step in the THA process is *Hazard Identification*. The team identifies hazards by "chair flying" their test events. They talk about normal test conditions and discuss the system design. In context, they determine the expected response and use their test experience to discover the potential hazards.

By design, there is no standard listing of hazards from which to select. The desire is for the team to go through the process. There

they examine each test as an unprecedented effort, with a fresh perspective.

Hazard

A condition prerequisite to a mishap or another incident resulting in damage to equipment, injury, or loss of life, or another adverse test impact (reduced effectiveness, efficiency, or test failure)

Example Hazard Types

Workload-induced
Over-tasking members of the test team which result in dropping essential tasks.

Situational Awareness
Causing a test team member to operate without full information regarding the environment that they are in.

System performance
Creating test conditions that exceed the system's capability, either designed or actual.

Process/Procedure
Steps or actions that when followed place the system or air vehicle in an unrecoverable state.

System knowledge
Not understanding the actual system design and unable to accurately predict the response.

Once identified, an examination of the hazard determines the most likely or most logical condition or circumstance leading to it. The team does not seek to find all possible causes for the hazard but instead find the one probable **cause** that would be emblematic of all of the other causes.

If the team identifies multiple, equally likely causes, they may decide to break the hazard into more than one entry for simplicity or track it with more than one cause. The team must decide if the cause and hazard are more likely to exist due to the test above that generally found in aviation. If so, they have a potential test hazard.

Cause

The reason for the hazard; either static (part of the environment or conditions), dynamic (due to the method or procedures), system-related (due to technology immaturity), or due to a deficiency (the system does not behave as designed or intended)

Next, the test team needs to find a **reasonable effect** resulting from the hazard. They attempt to complete the phrase "*encountering and experiencing the hazard will most*

likely result in [fill in the blank]." The goal is not to find all possible results, but only the one most reasonable and logical. The team must avoid stringing together multiple hazards and combining effects to inflate a hazard's significance.

If the team has difficulty in determining the cause or the effect, they should see if what they identified as a hazard better fits the definition of cause or effect. Misidentifying these items is relatively common, and the final answer is not the most critical part—it is the process that is important. *Note: Hazard, cause, and effect determination may be contentious in some teams.*

Effect

The likely result of a hazard, which has an adverse impact to test success (safety, efficiency, or effectiveness)

Once identified, the team determines the available and appropriate mitigation steps required to minimize the hazard to an acceptable level. First, the team identifies **precautionary measures** (or PMs) that reduce the risk likelihood.

Precautionary measures are specific steps taken either to (1) reduce the scope (thereby avoiding the hazard environment) or (2) modifying the method (thereby avoiding the hazard conditions). Either of these serves to lower the likelihood of realizing the hazard. Thus, PMs break the chain of events that links the cause to the hazard.

Precautionary Measure
Adjustment to test
scope or method to
(1) lower the likelihood of
realizing a hazard, or
(2) eliminate the possibility
of realizing it

Second, the team determines the available and appropriate **corrective actions** (or CAs) to break the chain of events that links the hazard to the consequence. Generally, CAs serve to limit the severity of the consequence (keep a bad day from getting worse). Some CAs can eliminate the most likely logical consequence, thus avoiding the risk entirely.

The test team should avoid chasing highly unlikely or unreasonable consequences as mitigation measures often become extremely expensive and cumbersome, sometimes preventing the test from effectively getting the required data.

Example Precautionary Measures (PMs)

- Removing a portion of test envelope to avoid a hazard
- Conducting additional pre-test inspection of the system under test in addition to the normal procedure
- Foreign Object Damage (FOD) inspection of taxi and takeoff area before, during, and after events
- Minimizing personnel during critical phases of test to remove distractions and improve situational awareness
- Test procedure walk-through or simulation to identify workload issues and provide familiarity
- Additional training and awareness of conditions that cause the hazard (increased system knowledge)
- Reduction of pilot workload by using chase aircraft
- Automated data collection systems in lieu of workload intensive manual data collection

Sometimes, the CA is published emergency procedure applicable to all flights in the test aircraft. In this case, the test team has identified a common aviation hazard. However, they chose to include it in the THA because their test profile led to increased exposure, which elevated the risk above a routine flight.

Application of an established emergency procedure may suffice to handle the hazard, and the test team simply incorporates the use of that procedure into the test method.

Corrective Action

Step taken to reduce or eliminate the consequence of a hazard, assuming that the hazard has been encountered

From the list of PMs and CAs that the test team has created to address the hazard, they select those that have maximum impact and minimal adverse effect on test integrity. Budget and time constraints also play a factor, as there may be measures or actions that would eliminate the risk but are unaffordable for the test program or prevent the team from collecting meaningful data.

The selection of appropriate and necessary PMs and CAs is an iterative process, where the CAs and PMs may influence each other, and the right mix needs to be determined. The goal is to reduce risk to an acceptable level. The team should not seek to eliminate all risk. Therefore, the team must systematically evaluate risks and determine when they are successfully handled.

Example Corrective Actions (CAs)

- Addition of back-up systems for test, such as brakes, parachutes, harnesses, lanyards
- Requiring Crash, Fire, and Rescue services available and standing by during high risk events
- Removal of live charges, devices, munitions
- Operations over unpopulated areas or open water to reduce chance of collateral damage
- Remote termination systems for unmanned aircraft to provide controlled crash
- Standard (or properly modified) emergency procedures

Test Hazard Realized

Even well-disciplined teams can experience a catastrophic event when a test hazard, whether known or unknown, is en-countered. Professional teams do not immediately assign blame, but instead follow a well-disciplined approach to de-termine the root cause, so that design or procedural im-provements can be incorporated to prevent future occurrenc-es.

During a regression test of a new software increment, the MQ-8B Unmanned Aerial Vehicle (UAV) experienced a hard landing that nearly destroyed the aircraft. The hard landing risk, due to a well-known design issue, was documented as a Test Plan THA.

The new software incorporated improvements designed to correct the issue, which only manifested itself during an au-tonomous or operator-commanded Launch Abort. The test team researched the improvements through the study of the design change documentation and consultation with the engi-neering team. It developed what was considered a low-risk test matrix to verify the corrections in software.

They planned three Launch Abort test points. On the first test point, the aircraft responded as predicted by getting light on the skids and then settling back down upon receipt of the Launch Abort command. However, during a repeat of the same test point moments later, the AV responded differently and lifted well off the ground, rapidly climbing to 8 feet before the Launch Abort command was received.

Then, the aircraft immediately transitioned to a "landed" state. The software commanded full down collective while still air-borne, resulting in the hard landing.

According to the software change documentation provided to the test team, recent corrections reduced the risk window for this previously-known problem to zero. Continued on next page

However, an investigation showed that the risk was only reduced from about 20 sec to 5½ sec following a launch command. Also, the Guidance, Navigation, and Control (GNC) system incorporated a rate integrator which continuously com-pared commanded rates to reported vehicle rates, and made flight control adjustments to match them. The difference be-tween the rates was called rate error.

On the first Launch Abort attempt, the rate error was zero. However, during the second attempt moments later, the residual rate error prompted a significant collective input. The GNC's attempt to correct for the residual rate error resulted in the unexpected takeoff before the abort and subsequent hard landing.

Following this analysis, the test team recommended that the GNC system set the rate error to zero after landing. Also, the test method was changed to account for the 5½ second window of vulnerability.

Improved cooperation between the test and design teams during test planning may have correctly assessed the risk and categorized it as unacceptable. The team would have altered the procedure (method change) or eliminated the test points (scope reduction). Either of these would have prevented the accident.

**Figure 13: Northrup Grumman
MQ-8B Fire Scout UAV**

The test risk management process requires a test team assessment and judgment to quantify the **residual risk** remaining after the **PMs** and **CAs** alter the **likelihood** and **consequence**.

Residual Risk

An expression of remaining loss in terms of likelihood of occurrence and severity of impact, considering the complete and correct application of the intended precautionary measure(s) and corrective action(s)

Likelihood

A qualitative judgment of the possibility of encountering a hazard during the intended test program (one flight or perhaps hundreds of flights)

A. **Frequent**
Most likely will encounter

B. **Probably**
Probably will encounter, but possibly will not

C. **Occasional**
Most likely will not encounter, but it is possible

D. **Remote**
Do not expect to encounter, although theoretically possible

E. **Not Possible**
Realization of the hazard has been eliminated and thus is no longer a THA item[16]

Consequence

A qualitative judgment of the severity of the impact of the most reasonable effect from hazard realization during the execution of the test as planned (i.e., with use of the intended corrective actions)

I. **Catastrophic**
Loss of the system or air vehicle; loss of life; anticipate termination of the test program

II. **Critical**
Significant damage to the system or air vehicle (or severe injury) resulting in a significant delay of the test program, missing milestone, or crucial deadline

III. **Marginal**
Damage to the system or air vehicle (or injury) resulting in delay to test program

IV. **Negligible**
Incidental damage to the system or air vehicle (or slight injury) not resulting in program delay

V. **No Impact**
The hazard no longer has a consequence and thus is no longer a THA item

Residual Risk Category

Two items are instrumental in flight test risk management. **First**, the test plan writer(s) must fold PMs and CAs back into the plan, so that they are not severable or separate, but integrated entirely into the scope and method. The THA items discovered and mitigated during the process are collected and inserted in a table, providing the cause, hazard, effect, PMs, CAs, and residual risk for each.

Second, the team assigns a residual risk category (Cat) for each THA, for test phases (collections of specific tests), and the test program (the most severe category for all tests). The NAVAIR process uses the residual risk categories shown in Figure 14.

The combined qualitative rating for likelihood and consequence determine the Test Risk Category associated with the THA item, and thus for the test event that generated the THA. Per the NAVAIR system, some residual risks are too high to proceed, or require additional discussion and work to handle.

Unacceptable risk brings a halt to test planning activities, as significant changes to test scope or approach are required to mitigate the hazard.

The approval authority does the final determination of the category for some risks as they weigh the factors in determining if Cat A, B, or C.

The benefit of folding PMs and CAs into the test plan is evident in that they serve to reduce the risk of the test program.

What is the significance of the residual risk category?

NAVAIR uses Risk Category to inform all in the organization rapidly (even those not involved in execution) as to the assessed risk for the test. Additionally, the test organization can set appropriate Search and Rescue (SAR) posture, environmental condition limitations (weather ceiling and visibility, winds, temperature), and required aircrew qualifications proportional to the residual risk.

Another advantage of test risk categorization is defining the roles and responsibilities within the oversight and approval process. Leadership delegates individuals with the responsibility to approve plans up to a specified category (e.g., Cat A and B only) while others may have unlimited authority (all Categories).

In this way, the THA process and the subsequent residual risk categorization may be used by the test organization as the foundation to the test risk acceptance system, enabling the test program to proceed with the necessary oversight, visibility, and overall buy-in from the organization.

		Severity			
		I Catastrophic	II Critical	III Marginal	IV Negligible
Probability	A Frequent	UA[1]	UA[1]	Cat C[2]	Cat B[3]
	B Probable	UA[1]	Cat C[2]	Cat C[2]	Cat A[4]
	C Occasional	Pause[5]	Cat C[2]	Cat B[3]	Cat A[4]
	D Remote	TBD[6]	TBD[6]	Cat A[4]	Cat A[4]

Figure 14: Residual Risk Categorization

Notes:

1. **Unacceptable (UA)**
   The risk too high to proceed with the test

2. **Category C**
   Significant risk to personnel, equipment, or property exists after taking precautionary measure(s) and corrective action(s)

3. **Category B**
   The risk to personnel, equipment, or property is *greater* than normal operations

4. **Category A**
   The risk is *no greater* than that seen during normal operations

5. **Pause (in Planning Process)**
   Pause for up-front discussions with test plan approver before continuing

   Note: The underlying test plan assumptions may be changed, so there is no reason to continue planning with the current assumptions.

6. **To Be Determined (TBD)**
   Coordination with test plan approver determines the final assignment of Category

Documenting Risk Mitigation

The test plan incorporates in several ways the outcomes from the various test team efforts to identify and mitigate test risks. The team embeds their thought process in every part of the plan.

The *background* contains relevant information from the previous testing that may include areas of concern that apply to current test risks detailed later in the plan. Additionally, the *description* of the system places particular emphasis on design aspects that require understanding to understand the risk.

The middle of the test plan, scope and method, have been re-worked from their initial shape to accommodate and include PMs and CAs determined by the THA process to be necessary and appropriate.

The test team shapes the test *scope* with precision to ensure that the air vehicle and system avoid risk areas considered too high or not necessary. Tailoring of the scope (applying limits) is tantamount to installing PMs, and the plan must balance them against the test objectives and data required from the test. The risk assessment may result in a limitation to scope that, in turn, limits the application of the results in the conclusion and recommendations.

The *method* section contains procedures that have been informed by the THA process and document how the test team intends to deal with topics, questions, and concerns contained in the safety checklist. The method must be sensitive to the limitations and restrictions presented in the flight clearance or airworthiness documentation.

The CAs from the THA process often find their way into the method as a restatement of currently established emergency procedures for the air vehicle or purposefully modified procedures (due to test article differences). The entire team (not just the pilot or UAV operator) should be responsible for knowing and understanding the importance of these procedures and how to execute them when required.

The *go/no-go* criteria documented in the Method section are a direct result of making risk-based decisions regarding the conduct of the flight. By providing the pre-planned responses, the test plan writers remove some of the burden from the test team to make these decisions under the pressures of flight test execution, increasing safety outcomes and reducing the chances of ill-informed decisions.

Some of the PMs and CAs from the THA process may have already been included in the first draft of scope and method sections due to the FTE's initial awareness of test risk and the basic principles and established procedures and practices for conducting a test.

Although the scope and method did not require a rewrite, the test team needs to make sure that there is consistency throughout the plan and that any information found in multiple places matches precisely. The effort to eliminate redundancy prevents confusion during test execution. The team consults different sections when making Data Cards or preparations for a flight (e.g., T&TC used for Data Cards, DMOT used for test flow, and THA table for pre-event brief). They must be consistent.

Finally, the *risk management* section itself contains a detailed listing of the THA items (typically in a table) and a completed SC. The team may choose to divide the THA table by individual tests, test events, and phases. Or, they may choose to list all THAs in one table for the entire test program, as required due to the length and number of items.

The table guides the pre-event brief, where the FTE or pilot reads each item aloud and discusses the specific measures and actions. This reminder ensures that awareness of the hazard and mitigation steps is uniform across the team and that the team's expectations are level.

If the test plan divides the THA table as described above, then only the items applicable to that day's events need to be briefed.

The SC, as described earlier, primarily serves a function in the test plan writing, review, and approval process by providing a guide to ensure that the test planning covered essential areas of concern. As far as documenting completion of the SC, the SC itself is typically included as an appendix and provides brief answers for each issue.

The answer may contain a reference to a page, chapter, or paragraph in the body of the plan that addresses the issue more thoroughly. Additionally, some writers include an extra step: in the body of the plan, where the issue is covered, they highlight the test (e.g., bold, italics, color font) and include a parenthetical reference to the SC number.

In this way, they have completed the cross-reference, allowing the reader to move back and forth from plan to SC with ease. Reviewers and approvers appreciate this technique since it makes their job a little easier. Test plan readers appreciate it as it helps them follow the test team's thought process.

The Scientific Method and Flight Test, Part II

"We had taken up aeronautics

merely as a sport.

We reluctantly entered upon

the scientific side of it.

But we soon found the work so fascinating

that we were drawn into it

deeper and deeper."

– Orville Wright

The Scientific Method and Flight Test, Part II

Returning to the scientific method and flight test: Step 4 Test divided into two parts: **First, Write a Plan** and **Second, Execute the Plan**. If done correctly, the test plan writing should be the hardest thing done during the test program. It takes the most time, the most energy, and assigns the most work. Each member of the team is busy researching ideas, studying the design, and documenting the results of their labor.

One experienced NAVAIR FTE established a personal rule of thumb:

> "for every day of flight test execution, expect a month of planning."

Of course, all generalizations break down at a point, but it is not too far off to assume that a week-long test event could take 6 months to plan.

> Planning should be the hardest thing done in Test.
>
> Proper planning makes test execution and reporting simple in comparison.

Step 4b. Test: Execute the Plan

Before putting the plan into motion, the test team must verify that they have satisfied the three-legged stool test: to work as a stool, there must be three legs. One or two legs do not make a stable platform.

Three-Legged Stool of Flight Test

The *first leg* of the flight test stool is the **Test Plan**. When signed, the document represents the authority to proceed and provides the entire organization's stamp of approval. A proper test plan ensures due diligence and application of the flight test discipline. The test plan addresses the three fundamental issues for the test effort:

1) What's the question?

2) How to get an answer?

3) What could go wrong?

The *second leg* of the flight test stool is the Airworthiness Certification or **Flight Clearance** (FC). The FC addresses the physical installation of the test system and leverages engineering analysis, discipline, and judgment in determining that the design is sound and adheres to physical principles and laws.

Three-Legged Stool of Flight Test:

1) Approved Test Plan
2) Documented Airworthiness
3) Configuration Management

Additionally, the FC provides instrumentation approval, covering the means, methods, and processes whereby the test team intends to collect data. Often the specific instrumentation clearances are received separately (in addition to) the FC for the system under test.

Finally, the FC declares the approved flight envelope within which the FTEs construct the test envelope. Receiving clearance for a new test envelope requires careful coordination between the FC authority and the test team, as the FC must be requested for the appropriate test scope and may lead to negotiation regarding how to properly (and safely) work within the scope.

The *third leg* of the flight test stool is **Configuration Management** (CM). This process is essential for several reasons, first that it provides documentation to describe the condition of the test article as tested. The test team must ensure to maintain those conditions per the CM process even during a fast-paced test program such as *fly-fix-fly*. Only this way will they be able to

associate results to specific design iterations and be able to track problem discovery and resolution through a convoluted timeline. Thus CM is directly related to the effectiveness and efficiency of a test program. Analysis can do little with data collected from the test article in an unknown configuration; the team might as well have not flown the flight.

The CM process ensures proper adherence to aircraft Weight and Balance (W&B). Air vehicles and flying machines continuously struggle with weight as they seek to master the laws of gravity. Balance is essential to maintaining control and stability as these machines aviate and navigate the skies. Failure to pay attention to proper W&B has resulted in numerous commercial, private, and military accidents during operational flights. Thus, it is incumbent on the test team to eliminate such accidents during developmental test flights.

Pre-Event Brief

To properly prepare for and execute a flight test event, the test team must conduct a pre-flight briefing with all of the members of the team present. Briefing attendees include support personnel who may not have participated in the planning process. It is the last chance to answer all questions, understand roles and responsibilities, and explain expectations.

The prudent team would conduct their briefing free from programmatic pressures and undue influence from outside, in part because they make hard decisions regarding actual test-day conditions and whether to proceed with the day's test event, pending meeting required criteria.

The briefing should cover the conduct and order of flight, including a review of the Test and Test Conditions (T&TC) for the event and the Data Cards, which they prepared to guide event flow and data collection efforts. The team examines the *go/no-go* criteria for the aircraft, equipment, and instrumentation, ensuring that

---

Pre-Event Brief

1) **Test objectives:** Goal of the event
2) **System configuration/loading:** Verify air vehicle and system are in expected condition
3) **Test points, methods, tolerances:** Specific tests from the T&TC table
4) **Knock-it-off criteria:** Conditions that result in suspension of the test point or event
5) **Limitations/restrictions:** Boundaries of the test envelop or specific methods to follow
6) **Backup test points/alternate:** In the event the primary objective cannot be accomplished
7) **Special precautions:** Additional points to emphasize
8) **THAs, project-related emergencies:** Review of applicable THA items and Corrective Actions
9) **Review of go/no-go criteria:** Verify that people, systems, conditions, and processes are ready
10) **No-vote philosophy:** Emphasize responsibility of each test team member to ensure safety

---

Importance of Designation

One of the critical tenets of the flight test discipline is that leadership does not base designations on position; they do not give them to someone simply because he or she occupies a box on the organizational chart. Leadership assigns flight test designations to individuals.

First and foremost, the individual must be knowledgeable of the flight test discipline and be credible in their proven execution. Flight test designations are progressive, with an entry-level designation given to someone who has gained the prerequisite *knowledge* of the discipline, a mid-level designation for those that have shown *ability*, and an advanced designation for those that have proven *skill* – knowledge, ability, and skill (KAS).

To be designated a Lead Test Engineer (LTE) is a great honor; one should not take them lightly.

---

everything is ready for the test event. Also, the team reviews the test day weather, atmospheric conditions, and system configurations for acceptability.

Finally, the team checks to make sure that each individual is ready for the job. These checks are more than just noting that bodies are present. Instead, the test team needs to ensure that the correct people are present (remember the **First Key to Successful Test**). The people ready to execute tests must possess current designations appropriate for the role that they have in the test (see **Importance of Designation**).

Several concepts and terms such as *No-vote* and *Knock-it-off* require a definition for use in the briefing and during test execution. *Go/no-go criteria* were explained earlier during the discussion of the Method section of the test plan.

No-vote

NAVAIR's test execution concept whereby all members of the test team are obligated to verbally request a stop to test when conditions exist that potentially adversely affect the safety of the test event.

The *no-vote* stays in place until those conditions are corrected or explained such that they no longer are a hazard, real or perceived. This philosophy is ingrained into all levels of test leadership and taken seriously by the organization.

Noone on the test team considers a *no-vote* lightly, but instead, they attempt to resolve it at the time through discussion and solve the issue in the mind of the one who issued the *no-vote* before resuming. But if the situation is not resolved in a timely fashion (i.e., while the aircraft is airborne with remaining test time and fuel), the team halts the test and resolves the problem with continued in-depth discussions.

Knock-it-off

Pilot-speak for stopping dynamic maneuvering and returning aircraft to a stable, static condition. The phrase can have several other meanings depending on context:

- **Formation maneuvering**
  Stop the engagement and separate the aircraft.

- **Test event**
  Stop taking data and recover aircraft before reaching a limit, e.g., attitude, airspeed, altitude).

- **Test flight**
  Complete data taking and return to base for landing.

It is essential to discuss terminology and how it is used during the day's flight so that all understand the communication.

Terminate

Another term that varies depending on context and background: order for in-flight destruction of a missile or UAS, discontinuing aerial dogfighting maneuvering (akin to *knock-it-off*), or some other agreed-upon signal.

Bottom line: the background and experiences of all involved in flight tests vary. For brevity and clarity, test teams often use terminology and code words. The pre-flight

---

A rule that states, "If something can go wrong, it will."

An addition to this law reads,

"and usually at the worst time."

– Definition of Murphy's Law
The New Dictionary of Cultural Literacy, Third Edition

---

briefing should include a review of the words part of the test team's lexicon and make sure that any new members of the team have a chance to learn their use and meaning before time is critical—because then it may be too late!

Test Execution

The nature of flight test is so incredibly diverse and varied that it would be impossible to document in this book every circumstance that would arise and what specific actions the test team should take. Instead, the focus has been on the discipline, including the primary tasks of test planning and test risk management. Given the vigorous debates, long hours, and critical thinking sessions that the team has encountered in the process of writing the plan, they are ready to execute.

Armed with the three-legged stool, prepared by a thorough pre-event brief, the team is ready for action. But one simple question to address first: *"Who is in charge?"*

A qualified and designated individual, called the **Test Director** (TD), typically performs test coordination duties. Other names for the TD may include coordinator, lead FTE, team lead, or some other variant.

Regardless of the name, the job of the TD is the same:

- Keep the efforts of team members coordinated during the event.
- Make sure that the test team members are fulfilling their roles and responsibilities.
- Assemble the data collected from the test and make sure that it is complete.
- Make sure that the instrumentation is functioning (with this, observe that SOT, SOF, and AC categories are recognized and followed).
- Use the framework of the test plan to guide real-time execution decisions for the team.

As the direct representative to the test plan approver(s), the TD must strictly adhere to the test plan, pre-event brief, and test cards *and demand the same from others.* If conditions drift outside of the bounds of the test plan, the TD must see it and call for a halt in the test event until the team can reassess the conditions per the guidance in the test plan.

If any member of the test team initiates a **No-vote**, the TD needs to respect that and ensure that the entire team is clear on intentions regarding how to proceed.

Several other test happenings may require the TD's attention. If there is a "Hold" or another delay for weather or other *go/no-go* criteria, the TD should brief the team and make sure to provide a time for reevaluating the conditions. With this, the TD needs to be aware of the length of the workday for team members, to ensure that fatigue does not adversely impact the test (refer to applicable SOP for guidance on leadership's expectations for the duration of the workday).

There may be range or resource scheduling issues that draw the TD's attention, requiring creative solutions to perform the test in light of diminishing or otherwise unforeseen changes to availability.

Finally, the TD (and the whole team) must be well versed in what to do in the event of a mishap or accident during the test. The TD reviews the procedures before the test, and rapidly takes charge and perform the required steps per the organization's Mishap (accident) plan. Acting as a liaison with authorities, coordinating communications with outside agencies, and controlling the activities of the test team post-mishap are essential functions that require the TD's attention.

Of course, the TD is not alone with all of these jobs and responsibilities.

The TD may delegate tasks to the members of the team, but the TD still maintains accountability to ensure they are done and done right. For example,s the instrumentation engineer should verify the proper function of the data collection and recording equipment. Still, if there was a failure and the test event lost due to a malfunction, it is the TD who answers for the oversight.

Similarly, it is the TD that leadership holds responsible for violations of the test plan. Leadership takes test plan exceedances very seriously, for they call into question professionalism and competence, and will no doubt affect the relationship with leadership and level of oversight for future tests.

Post-Event Debrief

The data are collected, the test flight is complete, the air vehicle put to bed, and the team is tired. But there are a couple of important tasks to be completed before moving on to the next test day.

At the post-event, the team must review the flight event they have just completed and ensure that there is a plan in place to use every piece of information learned. Top of the list of things to review are any **safety issues** seen during the flight.

Safety concerns from the test must be compared to the test plan THA items to see if any are new, invalid as initially written, or in need of revision. The TD should determine if there is a need to revisit the safety approach outlined in the test plan.

From this, the team may recognize **lessons learned** applicable to safety, effectiveness, or efficiency. The value of a lesson learned is not merely knowing about it, but in applying it to future events. Therefore, the team determines how best to make others aware of the lesson learned (if appropriate) and whether or not the issue requires an amendment to the current test plan (or can be implemented on future test flights within the current scope and method).

The data collected during the flight must be reviewed and checked. Any short-hand notes or scribble must be corrected and explained by the note taker. Comments made during the flight that had uncertain meaning need to be discussed and clarified. The quality of the data needs to be explained, including sources of error, ambiguity in the numbers, and the confidence that the data taker has in the source (if applicable).

The use of a *confidence factor* is a technique particularly helpful when taking a long series of connected data. If there are interim points in the data series with lower quality (e.g., the air vehicle had deviated from the planned conditions or strayed to the limits of the acceptable tolerance), they are

---

Post-Event Debrief

1) **Safety issues:** THA items seen, not seen, and new hazards not previously recognized
2) **Admin issues:** Ensure to complete post-flight paperwork and follow-up with support activities
3) **Review of data:** Clean up data cards, explain gaps, and define responses
4) **Deficiencies (and who will document):** Capture initial impressions and possible issues
5) **Lessons Learned:** Determine criticality and impact on current test effort, establish a plan to document and disseminate
6) **Action required prior to next test:** Create schedule, plan for data analysis, update records

assigned a low confidence. With the confidence factor, the team can continue to use the entire data set, recognize the errant points, and potentially apply corrections.

Without a confidence factor, the team would either have to throw out the entire data series or have an improper impression of the system performance.

The post-event debrief kick starts the next step in the scientific method (Analyze Results) and make sure that the raw material (collected test data) is ready. However, raw impressions readily apparent during the debrief are valid observations that should be collected and written down. More to follow below in these topics: Analysis, Conclusion, and Reporting.

Finally, the team must consider the administrative tasks required to complete the present day's test and get a start on the next. Coordination may be required with support facilities to let them know that the team finished their event and no longer needs their services that day. The test team completes that communication task along with a reminder of the next scheduled event that requires support services.

Step 5. Analyze Results

The data collected during the flight test represent facts about the system and its performance in the test configuration in the actual test environment. As such, these facts do not represent the system performance in the crucial three-fold state:

- In the intended environment,

- Employed by the end-user, and

- In operational conditions.

The first consideration for the test team is to verify that there was no possibility that a *maintenance discrepancy* impacted the results; in other words, that the system was not broken or otherwise unserviceable as compared to the designer's intent.

If the result was due to a maintenance discrepancy (i.e., burned-out lightbulb, faulty connector, cracked fitting, or corroded fastener) that does not necessarily let the system *"off the hook."* There still exists the possibility that a faulty design induced maintenance failure.

To examine this further, the FTE should consult reliability and supportability engineers who can help examine the data, look for trends, make conclusions, and recommend system corrections.

If, however, the test team determines that a maintenance discrepancy, malfunction, or another failure did not impact the test result, the team moves to the next layer of analysis. Here the team looks at the test result facts through the lens of the *Test Triangle*, seen in Figure 15.

The Test Triangle

When confronted with an unexpected test result (i.e., one that doesn't match the prediction), the FTE needs to consider these three possibilities:

First, the result is due to the test set-up and conditions.

In this case, the unexpected test result was due to a mismatch between the planned and actual test conditions. For an air vehicle, perhaps the state conditions of airspeed, altitude, angular rates, or accelerations were off. However, during software tests, there may

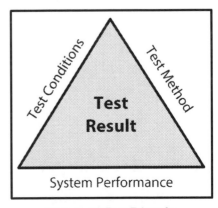

Figure 15: Test Triangle

have been residual values or conditions from the previous test, latch conditions, or some other unplanned input. The test team must analyze all data to ascertain whether or not the system was in the right conditions for the test.

An improper test set-up can occur for several reasons, but one the test team may encounter frequently is misunderstanding the system requirement and how best to test it.

When following the test plan set-up and method to verify a detection requirement for the MH-60R Airborne Low-Frequency Sonar (ALFS) acoustic system, the test team discovered that the system was not producing the predicted results.

The ALFS was internally-carried on the helicopter and lowered into the water to a predetermined depth from a stable hover. Once at depth, the sonar transmitted sound energy into the water and listened for the echoes returning from hard objects (contacts) in the water. But when tested, the system was not finding the contacts as expected.

Based on the performance of the ALFS system in individual engineering assessments, the power output, receiver sensitivity, range accuracy, and bearing accuracy all indicated that the system had the potential to outperform

expectations. When it did not, the test team was confused by the result.

Upon further analysis, the problem turned out to be the test set-up. The conditions presented to the ALFS resulted in a *"no detect"* score for the system during a scenario where detection was not possible (the contact was outside the theoretical range). Perhaps the tactics involved and the scenario as tested were at fault, but the test team attributed the result to a system deficiency.

Although it sounds obvious in this retelling, there was significant work to be done by the test team to explain their findings to all of the stakeholders and get an agreement with their proposed changes to the test set-up. They changed the test set-up to ensure that the ALFS was presented with valid detection opportunities, and then scored the performance of the system in those conditions. To validate their revised test technique, they included *"no detect"* trials in the test set-up, to ensure that the test operators were responding correctly.

Second, the result is due to the test method and approach.
Here, the conditions that the system encountered were correct, but the method used to obtain the data was wrong. Even under the best conditions, no system can respond as expected if tested with faulty methodology.

Instrumentation is generally considered part of the scope in test planning. The instrumentation list describes the dimensions of the data collected. However, the "test method" leg of the test triangle includes instrumentation.

How the team measured a parameter (method) caused the unexpected result, not the fact that it was measured (scope).

This phenomenon is related to the **observer effect** in physics (often confused with the **uncertainty principle**), which refers to changes that the act of observation makes to the item under observation.[17]

For example, checking the air pressure of a car tire lower the overall tire pressure, due to the small amount of air that escapes while measuring. Using a proper measurement technique minimizes the change to the tire pressure.

During a flight test, instrumentation may often rely upon aircraft power, air vehicle sensors and wiring harnesses, or physical switches, potentiometers, and position sensing devices that may impact the system. In other cases, test-compiled software loads designed to allow for visibility of threads and processes ordinarily transparent to the end-user may impact processor throughput, latency, and even accuracy.

For example, during a long duration ongoing test of diagnostic equipment on the SH-60B helicopter, the test instrumentation system required measurement of the engine turbine temperature to assess power performance.

The measurement was accomplished by tapping into the standard engine control wiring harness and reading the voltage from the engine thermocouples in the same way that the aircraft systems did.

Quite some time passed, and the team had flown many flight hours before they realized that the temperatures recorded on the instrumentation *and shown to the crew in the cockpit* were up to 20°C off due to the change in circuit impedance introduced by the instrumentation tap.

This error does not sound very large, but when testing engine performance, it can be very significant. The onboard engine control systems reduced available engine power based on turbine temperature limits, thereby compounding the temperature measurement error. The team unintentionally reduced the power available to the helicopter's rotor, but fortunately never encountered emergency conditions where every ounce of power was needed.

Third, the result is due to system performance characteristics.

Once the team rules out scope (test set-up) and method (procedure and measurement) as contributors to the unexpected result, the conclusion that remains is a test result due to a system performance characteristic. Thus, they must now process this test result *fact* or data into a conclusion about the system under test.

Normally one data point does not stand alone, so the datum is combined with others to build information regarding the performance of the test system under test conditions. But precisely what the test team does with this newly acquired information depends on the purpose of the test effort and the nature of the test question that they are attempting to answer.

Discovery

Information about system performance is collected and documented to understand the design features and how they work. Limitations to the capabilities are determined, and if significant (i.e., pose a threat to the successful completion of the intended mission), they are presented back to the designer for immediate consideration.

Verification

The FTE compares system performance characteristics to the drawings and design specifications. Then, the FTE documents the performance characteristics that possess corresponding system engineering requirements, and makes a factual statement regarding the comparison, using one of the following terms:

- **Exceeded**
  system performance was better than specified

- **Met**
  system performance was equal to that which was specified

- **Failed**
  system performance was worse than specified

Several items of note about verification:

1) Verification is not an evaluation of *"goodness"* or *"badness"* of the system. There is no valuation provided as the verification conclusion is a *factual statement*.
2) A *design failure* is a condition in which the system doesn't meet a parameter, typically a specification requirement.
3) Verification does not address *design intent*: the tester does not know whether the designer attempted to exceed the requirement, just meet it, or if the designer knew that the system would fail.

4) Meeting or exceeding design spec does not always indicate the system passes subsequent validation. The verification facts are additional data that the team may consider in the evaluation; however, the formal verification process has not considered mission relation or mission impact—the essential ingredients of an evaluation.

Characterization

Similar to discovery, but generally performed with proven technology and to a different degree. The focus is to take the test results and shape a useable operational envelope to inform Flight Clearance documents, Operator's manuals, and the like with accurate portrayals of the design's capabilities and limitations.

Since test events collect data under actual test-day conditions, often characterization requires a *generalization* of the results, which is using concepts and theory to guide reducing the *information* about performance from many conditions into a *knowledge* of performance under standard conditions.

Flight test teams use the concept of generalizing data often in air vehicle performance testing. For example, the goal of level flight performance testing is to determine engine power required and available vs. airspeed to create performance charts for the Operator's Manual. The team obtains data from the aircraft and environment at various altitudes, temperatures, humidity, and drag conditions.

The change in observed performance due to some of the variables is accounted for by theory: power available is a function of fuel flow, air temperature, humidity, and density (proportional to altitude).

Variations in these parameters are predictable, and corrections applied to compute the power available if the aircraft flew in the defined "Standard Atmospheric Conditions" or *standard day.* Likewise, the team computes power required and airspeed as guided by theory.

The result is **knowledge** of the level flight performance profile for flight in a *standard day,* even though the aircraft never flew in those conditions. The performance chart in the operator's manual is called **generalized** or **referred data**.

The pilots and engineers use the *standard day* charts to project performance to other-than-standard conditions and make conclusions as to how the air vehicle performs in a new operational environment. The projected results, called **unreferred data**, allow insight, which is of particular use in the next purpose of test, validation.

Test teams use similar techniques of *generalizing* test-day data to make conclusions for other-than-test-day conditions. These techniques apply to the testing of characteristics other than level flight performance, such as climb and descent performance and single-engine bingo profile.

The common theme throughout, however, is that proven theory and mathematical principles guide the generalization process. In all of this analysis, test teams must be aware of the limitations of the data that they have collected, so that they do not misuse it.

The most readily apparent improper use of test data is extrapolating into unknown regions of the envelope. *Extrapolation* requires holding to the assumption that the system continues to perform in the same fashion as the conditions change into untested regions. This assumption ignores real-world issues of limits, boundaries, inflection points, and knees in curves, and is generally an unwise test analysis technique.

Instead, the wise test team constrains their analysis to *interpolation* between their tested data points, where underlying assumptions of smooth continuous functions (while not always correct) are supportable.

System characterization brings up another essential test concept, one that feeds back into test planning. *Envelope expansion* is the process whereby the test team moves from known conditions outward toward unknown conditions. They do this methodically and carefully. The team must balance data collection, data analysis, and airworthiness considerations as they take the system into uncharted territory.

Close coordination between design engineer, airworthiness authority, FTE, and test pilot or UAV operator is required to proceed safely, efficiently, and effectively in any envelope expansion project. Note that the same principles apply to envelope expansion in other than air vehicle performance. The envelope expansion can be into a new electromagnetic environment, a new cyber environment, or some other area.

Validation

Perhaps if it were not for the need to perform flight both test and evaluation, all flight tests would be automated, and the human element removed. For it is in evaluation that the operational experience, time tested wisdom, and system, mission, and environmental knowledge of the test team comes together to analyze the test results in light of the mission relation to determine the effectiveness and suitability of the system for the end-user.

To restate the validation test objectives from earlier:

- Is the design the right one for the purpose?

- Does it properly operate in its intended environment?

- Does it meet the needs and wants of the end-user?

These three objectives assume that the test team understands the end-user's perspective and can judge the merits of the system performance in light of the end-user's expectations, needs, and desires. It is here when compared to the mission that a system may exhibit a *deficiency*, where it harms a successful mission or task accomplishment.

Because the deficiency adversely impacts mission accomplishment, the deficiency hurts the end-user. The deficiency prevents the operator from achieving success, they are required to exert unexpected or disproportionate effort to achieve success, their success may be partial, or they may be annoyed and frustrated by the system. All of these are valid results from the validation analysis that the FTE must document appropriately.

Bottom line: If there is no mission impact, then there is no deficiency.

Failure vs. Deficiency

You can have: and you can have

(1) A spec fail that is not a deficiency
(2) A spec fail that is a deficiency

However, you can also have

(3) A deficiency even while the system meets the specification

---

Step 6. Draw Conclusions

The sixth step in the scientific method is to conclude from test results and subsequent analysis. There are only a handful of conclusions that a flight test team makes from the data analysis they perform.

Sometimes the test team collects data and provides it to other agencies to analyze. In this case, when the other organization returns the processed information, the test team then "owns" the knowledge and can use it to draw their conclusions.

The test team's conclusions from *discovery*, *verification*, and *characterization* are the facts that they collect and document. However, evaluations (the primary tool of *validation*) yield conclusions on the effectiveness and suitability of the system for the end-user.

The primary conclusions from flight test split into two families: *satisfactory* and *unsatisfactory*, and then is followed by other conclusion categories that modify those two conclusions types.

Satisfactory
The system provides the end-user with an acceptable level of performance for mission accomplishment in the intended environment.

Note: A *satisfactory* conclusion follows the scientific method **"True"** decision path:

- The fundamental question of the flight test is answered
- The hypothesis of adequate, satisfactory, and correct system operation is confirmed
- The project moves to the final step in the scientific method

Unsatisfactory
The system exhibits a deficient characteristic that prevents, degrades, or otherwise adversely impacts mission accomplishment in the intended environment.

Note: An *unsatisfactory* conclusion is akin to the **"False"** decision path for the scientific method:

- The fundamental question of the flight test is answered
- The hypothesis of adequate, satisfactory, and correct system operation is defeated
- The system returns to design engineers for correction
- The redesigned system returns to the testers for a reevaluation, with a new hypothesis

Enhancing Characteristic
Some measured and evaluated system characteristics determined to be satisfactory exhibit qualities that beneficially impact mission accomplishment, resulting in

favorable outcomes beyond expectations or ways not anticipated in the original design. The test team may conclude that these **enhancing characteristics** are so noteworthy that they deserve formal recognition. The reasons for documenting them may be to inform the program manager or decision-maker about the beneficial quality or to ensure that the end-user is informed of the finding so that they can leverage the characteristic and take advantage of it in operations.

Frequently, enhancing characteristics are tangential to the intended design objectives. Therefore, the test team should exercise care and due diligence to verify the basic functionality of an item. Before consuming scarce test resources documenting a potentially unrelated (or un-asked-for) characteristic, the team must ensure that the system's design supports the intended purpose or mission. They must be confident that it is the right design for the right job before talking about the things that is wasn't intended to do.

An example of this occurred in the MH-60R radar test team. The helicopter's radar system included an Identification Friend or Foe (IFF) capability. The pilot uses the IFF Transponder when flying in controlled airspace. Additionally, the IFF Interrogator supported the helicopter's surveillance mission.

While testing the IFF, the team noticed that cycling the interrogator function repeatedly gave the crew incredible awareness of nearby aircraft. The system provided a display of altitude and navigation information for each aircraft in the sky, especially helpful when flying in congested airspace. The display essentially gave the aircraft an additional self-deconfliction capability—a poor man's Traffic Collision Avoidance System (TCAS), see Figure 16.

Sometime after writing up the **enhancing characteristic** in the test report, the program office learned from the Federal Aviation Administration (FAA) that the helicopter violated IFF interrogator design regulations. The FAA had figured out that the MH-60R helicopters operating out of NAS North Island in San Diego, CA were blanking the ground controller's screens in the Los Angeles Basin area.

The MH-60R IFF interrogator design exceeded the allowable Pulse Repetition Frequency (PRF) by several orders of magnitude. The exceedance meant that the system saturated the sky with electronic noise. Even though it was excellent at providing the helicopter crew information about the airspace (enhancing characteristics), the design deficiency resulted in FAA ground controllers repeatedly losing their situational awareness— *while controlling aircraft in one of the nation's busiest pieces of the sky!*

The US Navy directed the fleet pilots to stop using the feature that the designers had given to them (and that they were told was great to use) until the system could be redesigned and brought into compliance with regulations and design constraints.

In this example, the test team missed the requirement failure and reached the wrong conclusion. Fortunately, the only harm, in this case, was the pride of the test team involved, some embarrassment to the US Navy, and damaged relations between fleet helicopter pilots and FAA ground controllers.

Deficiency Categories

For most decision-makers or program managers, it does not suffice to inform them that the system is **unsatisfactory**. What they need to know is where this deficiency lies relative to other problems they are trying to deal with during the development.

Perhaps it is no surprise that there are issues affecting system effectiveness and suitability during developmental test. The trick is going to be what to do about them.

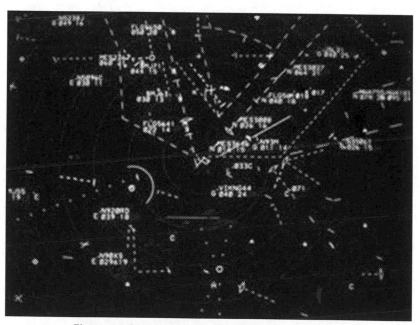

Figure 16: Representative IFF Interrogator Display

Since most programs do not have an infinite store of developmental resources, the test team must apply a priority or rank structure to the identified deficiencies. They do this when they make their test report to the program managers.

The names of the different levels of deficiencies vary depending on the organization, but what follows is a basic three-level structure patterned after NAVAIR's Part I, Part II, and Part III deficiency nomenclature. This list requires careful attention and crafting to make it appropriate to the systems under development. No list meets all flight test organization needs and must be considered flexible and negotiable. The deficiency level definitions may look radically different for an unmanned system compared to a manned system. It is a communication tool to be used between the test team and the audience to whom they ultimately report their results.

Critical Deficiency
The issue precludes mission accomplishment, presents a critical safety hazard, or requires excessive compensation by the end-user to overcome. Continued operations with this issue uncorrected ultimately lead to mission failure or loss of the air vehicle and people's lives.

Serious Deficiency
The issue negatively affects mission accomplishment and may prevent it unless the end-user applies compensation to correct; however, there is not a significant safety risk. Continued operations with this issue uncorrected are technically possible, but will make mission success more difficult and could result in damage to the air vehicle or injury.

Minor Deficiency
The issue presents a small challenge to the end-user and is not desirable. However, mission accomplishment is still possible, with a small level of compensation. The operator will be annoyed, but there is little risk for mission failure, damage to air vehicles, or injury.

As mentioned earlier, the test team's job is not complete merely with collecting data. Nor are they done once the data has been analyzed and assembled into coherent thoughts. Likewise, the team has not finished their job after offering conclusions. Only when they have informed their audience what to do about the conclusions are they complete with the test effort.

The team must provide the *So What?* with each test result. Recommendations must accompany conclusions. Without valid recommendations, conclusions are like a musical instrument without sheet music. Interesting to look at and touch, but incapable of creating the symphony and being complete.

Recommendations from a flight test come in two types: *general recommendations* and *specific recommendations*. A test report may include a mix of the two, described as:

General recommendations

Timing for the correction of the **deficiencies**. If there are no deficiencies, then the system is considered satisfactory. A timing recommendation for fixes is not appropriate (since there are no fixes to be made). Therefore, the general recommendation becomes a recommendation whether or not to move to (1) the next step in the development process (next DT&E phase), (2) operational test and evaluation (OT&E), or (3) operational use ("fielding" the system, in military-speak).

Specific recommendations

These can cover whatever the test team would like to happen in the case of an issue. It can include an approach or a means by which to mitigate, correct, or bypass the deficiency. The deficiency still exists even if the test found a suitable workaround—in that case, their recommendation could be to include the workaround as standard procedure for the system.

Step 7. Report Results

The final step in the scientific method is to report the results of the test. For flight tests, this expands based on the purpose of the test, and the question asked, to include reporting the results, mission impacts, conclusions, and recommendations. But before the test team can generate a test report with the answers to the questions asked of the test, they need to get one thing straight:

*Who is the audience
for this report?*

Know the Audience

As mentioned above in the section regarding the **Goal of Flight Test**, the nature of the decision must be understood. Additionally, the test team must recognize the position and role of its audience. In general, there are four types of audience members to whom the test team reports the results of the test.

1) **Design engineer**
   Interested in answers to facilitate design choices and corrections

2) **Senior-level management**
   Needs to understand the viability of the program (e.g., technical maturity and risks) to determine where to invest

3) **Program/project managers**
   Must verify requirement compliance for contract management (if applicable) or cost, schedule, and performance trades

4) **T&E professionals**
   Want visibility of test progress, methodology, and lessons learned (this includes members of the current test team who desire documentation of the work that they performed)

The point of the above is that it may be challenging to satisfy all of the various audience members with one report, and the test team should consider constructing documents to address the individual needs.

The design engineer may be able to get their best information from a sit down face-to-face discussion over the raw data and the test team's analysis notes and output.

Management may want a formal document for traceability or a verbal briefing with a softcopy of slides.

T&E professionals may want details of the test plan with insight into the scope, method, and risk (THA) to allow for test reconstruction and repeatability. Lessons learned from the test effort can be documented and distributed to others at conferences, seminars, verbal pass-downs, or inserted into the safety checklist.

Regardless of how the test team reports the data and the specific format used, there are some basic principles regarding creating a logical argument as the basis for communicating test findings.

Construct a Logical Argument

The flow of a logical discussion about test characteristics (enhancing, satisfactory, or deficient) resides in the time-tested NAVAIR approach called the **7-Part Paragraph**. That approach is summarized below.

Some parts are not applicable for enhancing (EC) or satisfactory (SAT) characteristics. Other parts are always optional. All are shown below, marked for their applicability, and given with a **hypothetical example**.

1. **Test and Test Conditions**
Name the test performed to enable the examination of the characteristic. If no one test applies, then name the characteristic. Detail the relevant (and significant) test conditions. Typically these include:

- Configuration, with software version (as needed)
- Gross Weight for air vehicle
- Atmospheric conditions
- Location of the test
- Time/date of the test

The report should state the test conditions as concisely as possible, ensuring that the reader does not see any glaring holes in the information ("this says that *climbing performance* was deficient—but how much did the test article *weigh*?").

Another part of the Test Conditions relays what the test team *expected* from the system when tested under those conditions.

Test & Test Conditions

The vertical climb performance of the Mark I Lawn Chair Cruiser was tested in the standard configuration with 21 balloons, 2 cup holders, and 3 sandbags. With the pilot and ballast onboard, the total gross weight was 250 lbs. Winds were calm, and the sky was clear with 75% humidity. The launch was from my backyard at 123 Maple Avenue.

Mark I Lawn Chair climb performance was expected to ex-ceed 1000 fpm to safely reach working altitude before being noticed by my neighbors.

---

2. Results

(always required)

Report the test findings in the most straightforward language possible, removing all extraneous details that cloud the issue for the reader. The test team is professionally responsible for being concerned with the secondary effects and contributing issues. The reader wants to rapidly understand what the issue is and what to do about it.

Often the results section is complete at this point. Sometimes there needs to be more information given to explain what the results meant to the test team as they were experiencing it to prepare the reader for the next step, which is to explain why it matters to the end-user.

3. Mission Impact (MI)

(not required for SAT)

Given the test conditions, expectations, and results, the test team must develop the mission impact for what will definitively occur for the end-user. The MI should reference the mission, safety, or other factors such as effectiveness, suitability, workload, and situational awareness.

Mission Impact is the most critical part of the report. It must be reasonable and supported by documented data. The MI may make a few logical, short steps to show the significance of the deficiency, but the team must guard against assuming that the reader can fill in gaps and follow a giant leap from one idea to the next. Make it simple, easy to follow, and (above all) make it inescapable.

Results

Upon lift-off, the chair reached 500 ft in 72 seconds. When the chair passed through 1000 ft, a total of 167 seconds had elapsed, resulting in a climb rate of 360 fpm through the first 1000 ft.

My nosy neighbor heard me counting out the seconds as I climbed and the last thing I saw he was dialing a phone. I thought that I was going to get caught this time.

Mission Impact

The pathetic vertical climb performance of the Mark I Lawn Chair Cruiser will result in getting tracked by the FAA, intercepted by the US Air Force, and thrown into jail for 5-10 years.

---

4. Conclusion

State whether the characteristic is enhancing, satisfactory, or deficient. If deficient, list the level of the deficiency. Also, give the general recommendation (timing of the correction) for deficient characteristics.

5. Cause Analysis
(optional)

Not a place for conjecture, the Cause Analysis is the test team's best-educated engineering judgment as to the nature of the cause. If unknown, do not offer a guess and simply skip the section. Otherwise, help program management or the design engineer know where in the design to look for the correction.

6. Specification Compliance
(optional)

If there is an applicable specification or another requirement that addresses the characteristics, then the compliance fact of exceeded, met, or failed is listed. Otherwise, nothing.

7. Specific Recommendation
(optional)

Provide any applicable specific recommendations, such as how to fix the problem or whether to retest to gather more information.

Conclusion

The pathetic vertical climb performance is a Critical Deficien-cy which must be corrected before the next test flight (or I'll be a goner!).

Cause Analysis

This deficiency is most like due to the extra 20 pounds that I put on over the holidays.

Specification Compliance

The vertical climb performance of the Mark I Lawn Chair Cruiser failed the FAA vertical climb in Class G airspace requirement in that the vertical climb rate of 360 fpm was 140 fpm less than the minimum 500 fpm (28%).

Specific Recommendation

Consideration should be given to following up with doctor's recommendation for exercise and watching what I eat.

Make it Easy for the Reader

Following a logical-argument template sounds easy, but it takes practice and patience to make it work. The trick is to identify what each piece of information is and place it in the right location. Once the argument flows well and reads quickly from step to step, the writer removes the paragraph header and combines all seven (or whichever sections used) into one paragraph, being careful to leave them in the correct order and close up the gap around sections not used.

The result is a report paragraph that is an easy read for the audience, that flows logically from one step to the next, and that gives them the information that they need to take action.

Other Types of Reports

Since the test program sponsor had a question and provided resources to the test team to enable them to perform a test to determine the answer, they desire a report of some type to give them the answer. The test report described above fulfills the fundamental need for a report of test results.

But there are other types of reporting that the sponsor (referred to here as the program manager) may want throughout the conduct of the test.

Status Report

Since the program manager has provided the test team with a system for evaluation, funds to pay for it, and other resources, it makes sense that they would want a status update to see how the test program is proceeding. The goal of the update is to give the most amount of information in the minimum amount of time.

There is a handy format that the team can use to write a status report. It is called "**EFAR**" and comes from the format of a military situation report (SITREP). **EFAR** stands for:

E – Enemy/Enemies

F – Friendlies

A – Administrative Needs

R – Request Assistance

When asked for an update, the answer is simply formatted as follows:

E – Enemy

While there may not be an *Enemy* encountered during a test program, the first section describes the challenge, problem, or phase in which the team is currently involved. Resource challenges, system troubleshooting, or the current test serial numbers (out of a larger plan) can work to start the conversation in a status report. This start lets the reader know what the topic is for the remainder of the report.

If there are multiple **Enemies**, the team should break the report into two separate updates. As unique issues, the team deals with one at a time and prevents the reader from combining them in their minds. The risk is that the reader may assume multiple issues resolved when completed actions only corrected one.

For example, while testing the MH-60R ALFS (see the sidebar on page 27), both Transducer Array (TA) assemblies (the part of the sonar that lowered into the water) malfunctioned and needed to be fixed by the manufacturer. They were sent overseas to Thales for repair. However, they did not return to the test team when expected. The preliminary investigation revealed that they were missing in transit when shipped by Thales back to the test team. Stymied by the situation, the test team decided to update the program office an update and bring additional resources to bear.

The missing TAs and ensuing delay was the **Enemy**, as written in the opening of the **EFAR** report, titled "**Issue**" as shown in the box below.[18]

F – Friendlies

The second section in a status update identifies the **Friendlies**. These are the people, processes, and resources engaged in dealing with the identified **Enemy**. If needed, this section may list the test team members, with their role or responsibility. Also, **Friendlies** may include other organizations contacted regarding the problem or issue.

EFAR Status Report

Issue:

The ALFS test program is on hold, as both test Transducer Array assets are missing. They were lost during transit to the test squadron after repair at the manufacturer's facility in France.

Points of Contact:

The ALFS manufacturer and the MH-60R prime integrator have been notified about the problem. The resolution team for this issue includes:

- *Test Team POC:*   *Jane Doe (555) 555-0101*
- *ALFS Manufacturer POC:*   *Jean Dupont (123) 456-7890*
- *MH-60R Logistics POC:*   *Joe Schmoe (098) 765-4321*

continued on next page...

Returning to the example with the missing ALFS TAs, the *Friendlies* section of the EFAR may look like that shown in the box on the previous page, labeled "**Points of Contact**."

Note that the status report segregates the *Friendlies* into a bulletized or numbered list to give clarity. The reader sees the organizational boundaries between the entities, and had a handy list should they desire follow-up or more information on the subject of the status report.

A – Administrative Needs

The third section of the **EFAR** is very flexible and contains the bulk of any discussion, background, or conclusions about the matter. Generally, the *Admin* section states what actions the team has taken and, if known, what their next steps are. Additionally, *Admin* may include any foreseen delays, projected resolution dates, or planned follow-up actions.

The intent of the status report is not to ask for input, detail every thought involved in addressing the issue, or clouding the matter in the nid of the reader. It should be straightforward and definite, without distractions and alternatives. If the team has not yet settled on a plan of action, then the status report should not be a list of the options the team faces or all items under their consideration. Instead, the status report should declare that a decision is pending, along with *when* and by *whom*.

The example *Admin* section details *who* has taken *what* action and *what* presents a barrier to action. In the example shown below, the section is titled "**Discussion**."

EFAR Status Report   (continued)

Discussion:

A worldwide trace initiated by the shipper was negative. The last known location of the crates was onboard a cargo con-tainer ship that left the Port of Le Havre in France, bound for Port of Baltimore, due to arrive two weeks ago.

Without test assets, the ALFS test program will slip day-for-day and not complete on schedule. The test team has added a second crew to accelerate the test schedule when testing resumes. This requires funding and coordination of extend-ed operating times with the range facility.

continued on next page...

R – Request Assistance

The last section of the **EFAR** is the most important. Here the writer provides specific and actionable requests to the reader. These requests should be discrete and within the power or influence of the intended recipient. It does no good to ask for something that the reader cannot provide!

Each request should be bounded. Bounded means that the reader should be able to perform the request and know when they are complete. The status report is not the right way to ask for ongoing or perpetual support. Instead, that is a CONOPS or a process change that should be negotiated and discussed before implementation.

If the status report omits this last section, the test team faces a risk with two highly likely outcomes. They may receive zero assistance; thus, they remain in the same situation as if they had never written the status report. Or, equally problematic, they receive the wrong help—precisely what they did not need, however enthusiastically offered.

In the final piece of the complete example **EFAR**, shown in the box below, Request Assistance provides the reader with two specific actions. Both imply further conversation once the reader initiates the actions. If they find the TAs at the customs office, the presumption is that they let the POCs (shown earlier in the report) of the findings. Also, if the reader decides to act on the request for additional range time, the "coordinate" request implies further discussion.

An **EFAR** format is flexible. It can serve as the basis for an extended discussion and report spanning several pages. On the other end of the spectrum, the team can use a streamlined **EFAR** to give a four-sentence reply to an email.

EFAR Status Report (continued)

Request Assistance:

1) Request that the program office contact the US Customs Office in Baltimore, MD, to determine if the TAs are there.

2) Additionally, request the program test & evaluation manager coordinate with the range scheduler to secure ex-tended test range time to complete testing upon receipt of the TAs and resumption of the test program.

One last important note regarding status reports: they do not include test results, conclusions, or programmatic recommendations. The status report is not a substitute for Test Reporting. It is provided to the test sponsor either at a predetermined interval (a periodic status update) or as situationally dictated. Finally, the test team can also produce a status report on demand-when the test sponsor asks for one!

Deficiency Report
During test execution, when a test finding demands it, the test team can send results, conclusions, and recommendations to the test sponsor with a *deficiency report*. A properly-written deficiency report contains only one deficiency, typically found regarding one system or air vehicle characteristic. The reason for sending the deficiency report to the program sponsor is to allow for rapid action. During developmental testing, there are many problems found and resolved. The deficiency report is a crucial communication tool used in that process.

The deficiency report looks much like the logical, structured 7-part paragraph presented earlier (Step 7. **Report Results**, page 120-123). However, the deficiency report does not convey *satisfactory* results or *enhancing characteristics*; thus, it is explicitly shaped for *unsatisfactory* characteristics. As such, it contains the following items, at a minimum:

1. **Deficiency Title**
   What is the technical issue that demonstrated the deficiency?

2. **Test Conditions and Results**
   What was done during the test, what the team expected to find (prediction), and what they did find (results)?

3. **Mission Impact**
   Why does it matter? How does the problem affect mission completion, safety, or the correct operation of the system?

4. **Conclusion/Recommendation**
   What is the priority of the problem relative to other issues with the system under test? When is a resolution needed?

5. **Cause Analysis**
   Why the problem occurred (if known)?

6. **Specification compliance**
   How does the system performance compare to the requirements and the designer's intent?

7. **Specific Recommendation**
   Are there any discrete actions to take in correcting the problem?

The more important or significant the problem is, the quicker the test team should report the issue via a deficiency report.

Quicklook Report

Occasionally, a problem arises during testing that needs immediate attention and discussion. When this happens, a *Quicklook Report* may be appropriate.

The Quicklook report may be accompanied by a face-to-face briefing, that allows the team to go into more detail than that which fits in a deficiency report.

Another use of a Quicklook is to combine several results into a summary of findings for one particular aspect of the system. The aspect could be a specific mission area, task, or piece of the overall CONOPS. The reason for the Quicklook may be that the program sponsor has an acquisition decision to make during the development of the system, and needs a system performance appraisal to support the decision.

The format of a Quicklook varies. It may consist of a written report combining several of the elements shown above in a full test report, status update, and a deficiency report. It may even be a presentation, delivered in-person, via video conference, or by phone.

Regardless of the format, the Quicklook gives the same thing that all test reports do: results containing data, conclusions supported by the results, and recommendations based on the conclusions. Any test report that does not lead to conclusions and recommendations is simply organized data, and not useful for decision making. The organized data still needs interpretation and analysis, which is what the test report, deficiency report, or Quicklook report provides.

Interim Report

The last type of test report mentioned here is the *Interim Report*. As the name implies, it is not the final report! If the test program sponsor needs an update on the results of the test, good and bad (satisfactory and unsatisfactory), they can not look at a *deficiency report* alone. They only give bad news. A *status report* from the test team does not give test results, conclusions, and recommendations. Lastly, a *Quicklook* report may be too narrowly focused and fail to provide the reader with a complete overall impression of the system performance.

The interim report is not a fast version of the *final report*. There may be items left out of the interim that the test team includes in the final test report. But the interim report serves its purpose: give the program sponsor a snapshot of the overall findings (to date) during an extended flight test program.

So What?

The reason to test is simple: designers, developers, and managers of sophisticated aircraft, systems, and components need information on the performance of the systems they build. They need to understand two things:

Does the system match the design intent? Is the system built right?

Does the system do what we need it to do? Is the right system?

Answers to these questions are required to allow **decision-making** during the design, development, and fielding of these systems. Those decisions center around the three-fold constraint at the center of the program manager's job: **cost**, **schedule**, and **performance**.

Just as the "man behind the curtain" in The Wizard of Oz manipulated controls on a panel to put on the illusion of the Wizard, the program manager (though without the negative connotation from the movie) manipulates money/cost, time/schedule, and requirements/performance to produce a working system for the end-user. Money and time are straightforward: the manager adds or subtracts money from the effort (by moving the lever of contracts or direct investments), or accelerates/decelerates the development timeline (by moving the calendar dial of scheduled events, meetings, and deadlines).

But it is the last of the three: performance; that presents the biggest challenge. There is no lever, knob, or switch that dictates the system performance. Instead, the manager commissions the test team to discover, verify, characterize, and validate the performance, and then report their findings. These tasks are the job of the flight test engineer, pilot, and operator, who together comprise the flight test team. Their job is ever-changing, never twice the same, and full of surprises. It requires innovation, imagination, and discipline.

The flight test discipline continues to evolve with the complexity of the systems we test and the tools we have to test them. Nevertheless, the necessary foundations of flight test remain timeless. It is up to the practitioners of flight test, armed with critical thinking, to apply the fundamentals in ways that keep pace with the rigors demanded by modern aviation to ensure safe, efficient, and effective flight test.

End Notes

1   Shupek, John, The Skytamer Archive. Skytamer.com, Whittier, CA, retrieved August 26, 2016, from http://skytamer.com/1904.html

2   Lilienthal, Otto, Birdflight As the Basis of Aviation: A Contribution Towards a System of Aviation, First edition, 1911, Reprint edition, Markowski Intl, January 2001. ISBN 0-938716-58-1.

3   Wikipedia contributors. (2020, March 3). Otto Lilienthal. In Wikipedia, The Free Encyclopedia. Retrieved March 5, 2020, from https://en.wikipedia.org/w/index.php?title=Otto_Lilienthal&oldid=943731260

4   http://www.todayinsci.com/L/Li-lienthal_Otto/LilienthalOttoQuotations.htm, retrieved August 26, 2016.

5   XB-70 Valkyrie Mid-air collision June 8, 1966, Youtube, https://youtu.be/fCORwUxlNQo

6   F-18/A-4 Midair Collision, Youtube https://youtu.be/LBqm7asYs6Y

7   The program spent approximately $13M in support of this particular test methodology, and the final data collected included about 215 data points, each representing a 15-minute cycle of the system under test. Flight test programs are expensive!

8   Rees, Peter, creator, MythBusters, Discovery, 2003-2016.

9   Wikipedia contributors (n.d.), Scientific Method. In Wikipedia, The Free Encyclopedia. Retrieved August 28, 2016, from https://en.wikipedia.org/wiki/Timeline_of_the_history_of_scientific_method

10   Wikipedia contributors (n.d.), Scientific Method. In Wikipedia, The Free Encyclopedia. Retrieved on August 28, 2016, from https://en.wikipedia.org/wiki/Alhazen

11   As cited in https://en.wikipedia.org/wiki/Roger_Bacon, retrieved August 28, 2016: Bacon, Opus Majus, Bk.&VI.

12   Wikipedia contributors (February 6, 2020). Scientific method. In Wikipedia, The Free Encyclopedia. Retrieved March 5, 2020, from https://en.wikipedia.org/w/index.php?title=Scientific_method&oldid=939491171

13   Although the acronyms V/STOL and STOVL are similar, they represent different approaches to entering/exiting powered flight.

14   See   http://myweb.tiscali.co.uk/hawkerassociation/hamain/wheelmis fortune.html for a description of the "V/STOL Wheel of Misfortune," which lists 45 different aircraft (excluding helicopters) though the years which attempted success. According to the author, "only 3 have led to operational aircraft." Entry of the Joint Strike Fighter into service in 2015 made that total 4, with one to be retired soon, the AV-8B Harrier.

15   https://en.wikipedia.org/wiki/Lock-heed AH-56 Cheyenne,   retrieved August 28, 2016.

16   Although eliminated, the test team may want to include a discussion of the hazard in the test plan so that the reader understands the rationale behind the embedded precautionary measures in the plan addressing the risk.

17   Wikipedia contributors (February 6, 2020). *Observer effect*. In Wikipedia, The Free Encyclopedia. Retrieved September 5, 2016, from https://en. wikipedia.org/wiki/Observer effect (physics)

18   The reader should know that this example is a highly fictionalized account based loosely on a true event. The TAs were indeed missing for a short time and rapidly recovered once the team identified the issue to the program office.

Glossary

Selected flight test related terms and concepts used in **Flight Test: The Discipline** with expanded contextual definitions. In flight test, as with other disciplines, ***words mean things!***[1]

Ability. Demonstrated conversion of knowledge into action, in particular practices in the science and art of test planning, execution, and reporting.

Acceptance test. A specific test designed to confirm that the system meets the contractual design requirements. Completion of an acceptance test generally precedes the transfer of a completed item from designer/builder to the requester and often allows for contractual payment or closeout. For aviation systems, the *acceptance test* may include lab, ground, and flight tests, as required.

Air Vehicle. Agnostic reference to the host aircraft, includes rotary-wing, fixed-wing, and any other ***heavier-than-air*** flying machine. Often the aircraft itself is the ***system under test***, but when it is not, the term *air vehicle* refers to the host aircraft. Flight test evaluates integrated systems individually, collectively, or together with the *air vehicle*.

Airworthiness. Per the Federal Aviation Administration (FAA), "*Airworthy* means that the aircraft conforms to its type design and is in a condition for safe operation."[2]

Allocated baseline. Description of the system created by distributing the required functionality among the individual components, assemblies, and sub-systems that comprise the overall system (system engineering).

Analysis Critical (AC). Instrumentation category to indicate that the parameter is a required outcome of a particular test event to determine the answer(s) to the test objectives.

---

[1] Rush Limbaugh, February 18, 1994, Undeniable Truths of Life #34, as presented at The 'Lectric Law Library, http://www.lectlaw.com/files/cur52.htm, retrieved 3 Sept 2016.

[2] http://www.faa.gov/regulations_policies/handbooks_manuals/aircraft/amt_handbook/media/FAA-8083-30_Ch12.pdf, retrieved September 3, 2016.

Assumption. The substitution of engineering estimates/generalizations for information that is not fully known until the actual information can be obtained (if necessary); in flight test, all *assumptions* increase test risk.

Aviate/Aviation. The actions and processes involved with controlling an air vehicle in flight.

Bench test. See **Laboratory test**.

Black Box. Test approach where the test team does not have an insight into the inner workings of the system and, therefore, only can interact with the system through setting input conditions and observing the output.

Build-up. Test method for progression from a benign condition incrementally towards an unknown/severe point. *Build-up* can allow the pilot/operator to practice and get ready for the final point or can be used to exercise the data collection, monitoring, and procedure used by the entire test team.

Cause. The test team's assessment of what part of the design is contributing to deficiency or non-compliant performance based on system knowledge and direct observation during flight tests.

Characterization. A level of flight test where the objectives include understanding and documenting the full range of the system capability, potentially with limited expectations or predictions pre-test.

Critical Thinking. "Engineers concerned with good thinking routinely apply intellectual standards to the elements of thought as they seek to develop the traits of a mature engineering mind."[3]

Communicate/Communication. The actions and processes involved with coordinating air vehicle operations with other aircraft or ground controller stations.

Concept of Employment (CONEMP). A high-level description of daily system use vice a specific sortie or mission profile, often showing relationships with other systems, interoperability issues, and interfaces.

---

[3] Elder, Linda and Paul, Richard, Critical Thinking Concepts & Tools, Foundation for Critical Thinking, 2009.

Concept of Operations (CONOPS). A discussion that focuses on how the system would be operated to accomplish the end-user's objective, often combining environmental and mission combinations into a hybrid scenario or profile.

Conclusion. The outcome of an analysis of test results about characteristics that have a mission relation intended to provide knowledge of how the system performs for the end-user in the operational environment.

Concurrent test. Test methodology which combines multiple test objectives into one test flight. Typically one test is the primary objective, and the other is the secondary or "ride-along" test objective. The secondary test works well if it is low risk and not operator intensive.

Configuration Management (CM). The practice of understanding and controlling design changes to a system under development. *Configuration management* is required to ensure that the test team maintains the system in a known condition for a test.

Contractor test. Flight tests performed early in the development of a system, typically focusing on **verification** and **acceptance** activities.

Corrective Action (CA). Action, procedure, or process implemented in a test plan intended to reduce the severity of a consequence after the realization of a test hazard.

Daily Flight Report. An essential test event work product that includes details about (1) test team observations and impressions, (2) the collected data, (3) any lessons learned, (4) the test conditions, and (5) the results. The *daily flight report* provides the raw data for the analysis and final test report generation.

Data. Discrete quantitative or qualitative pieces of information that come from the system response or system performance when operated within known or controlled conditions.

Data cards. Test execution tools designed for data collection, event prioritization, process reminders, procedures checklist, and test script for all team members; constructed from the information in the test plan.

Deficiency. An identified characteristic of the **system under test** that presents a detrimental impact on the successful completion of the desired mission or task by the end-user in the intended environment; the severity of the impact assists the test team in determining the recommended course of action for correction.

Design of Experiments (DOE). "A series of tests in which purposeful changes are made to the input variables of a system or process and the effects on response variables are measured."[4]

Detailed Method of Test (DMOT). Test plan appendix providing procedures and descriptions of non-standard or unique test set-up and execution for the tests contained in the plan.

Determine. Test objective to find one or more characteristic performance values from the system under specific conditions.

Developmental Test & Evaluation (DT&E). "Engineering-type tests used to verify the status of technical progress, verify that design risks are minimized, substantiate achievement of contract technical performance, and certify readiness for initial operational testing."[5]

Discipline. Pertinent definitions from Merriam-Webster: "3: a field of study" and "6: a rule or system of rules governing conduct or activity."[6]

Discovery. A level of flight test where the objectives include experimentation with the system to witness operations and outputs in new environments or under new conditions.

Dissimilar Formation. Flight maneuver that requires two or more different aircraft (not the same type/model) to fly together, where the pilot community does not have established standard practices, procedures, and sightlines.

---

[4] Telford, Jacqueline K., *A Brief Introduction to Design of Experiments*, Johns Hopkins APL Technical Digest, Volume 27, Number 3, 2007, accessed at http://www.jhuapl.edu/techdigest/TD/td2703/telford.pdf, retrieved September 3, 2016.

[5] Per DT&E definition, Defense Acquisition University https://dap.dau.mil/acquipedia, retrieved September 3, 2016.

[6] Merriam-Webster online dictionary, http://www.merriam-webster.com/dictionary/discipline, retrieved September 3, 2016.

EFAR format. Adapted from a military situation report (SITREP), the *EFAR* format consists of four paragraphs:

E – Enemy
F – Friendlies
A – Administrative Needs
R – Request Assitance

Effectiveness/Effective. Statement of system capability to be used in a manner to achieve the desired outcomes.

Efficient. Regarding the aim of the test planning process, the degree to which the test uses resources in a way to gain the best, most complete test answer without unnecessary expenditure of time or money.

Effective. Regarding the aim of the test planning process, the measurement of success relative to entirely and thoroughly answering the test question(s) with appropriate confidence and accuracy.

End-user. The individual or group employing the system to gain the designed capability; when capitalized generally refers to the final recipient of the system (thus excluding test team), otherwise any (including test team), also referred to as *Operator*.

Enhancing Characteristic. Satisfactory quality of the *system under test* that beneficially impacts mission accomplishment, resulting in favorable outcomes beyond expectations or ways not anticipated in the original design.

Envelope expansion. The process whereby the test team moves from known conditions outward toward unknown conditions. The *envelope expansion* process is used to "clear" the *envelope* for airworthiness certification purposes, ultimately resulting in the defined operational *envelope* for the system end-user.

Environment. The general description of the conditions in which the system is operated, including external factors such as atmospheric ambient and electromagnetic/acoustic background levels, and internally-generated factors such as linear and angular rates and accelerations.

Evaluate/Evaluation. Test objective to assess the effectiveness and suitability of the system for a specific (defined) mission or task expectation.

Exceeded. Statement of fact regarding the *system under test*, as compared to the specification during *verification*: system performance was better than specified.

Experiment/experimentation. Program by which a technological approach or new method is subjected to operations in controlled conditions to observe utility or application, typically with less structured data collection and rigor as for flight test & evaluation.

Extrapolation. Projection of system performance outside of the bounds of collected test data. Assumptions regarding how performance varies outside of the known limits guides the *extrapolation* effort, which may contain significant errors if those assumptions are faulty. The FTE typically avoids *extrapolation*, as the ensuing results are low quality, have little confidence, and are not reliable for decision making. See **Interpolation**.

Failed. Statement of fact regarding the *system under test*, as compared to the specification during verification: system performance was worse than specified.

Flight Clearance. Airworthiness documentation provided by a technical authority permitting flight operations of the system under delineated conditions (flight envelope) and configuration, with listed restrictions.

Flight Control Description (FCD). A detailed discussion of the *air vehicle* control system, tracing control axes, motion paths, and channels through the design.

Flight Readiness Review (FRR). A deliberate determination that the *system under test*, and the air vehicle wherein it resides, is safe and ready to proceed to a flight event. The *FRR* does not necessarily consider the functionality and operation of the system (i.e., it may not be mature and complete working), but instead focusses on risks and hazards that the system presents to safe flight operations (aviate, navigate, communicate).

Fly-Fix-Fly. System development/maturation concept with rapid, immediate correction of deficiencies and problems between test flights; not appropriate for systems that impact basic airworthiness or safety.

Functional Baseline. Description of the system created by listing the individual capabilities the system must provide to meet the user's overall capability need (system engineering).

Generalized data. Results collected under test-day conditions, transformed into the equivalent value as if the test team collected the data under standard (or defined) condition. Physical relationships and mathematical principles/concepts guide the *generalization* process. Also called *referred data*.

Go/No-Go **criteria.** Conditional statements that indicate actions to be taken under defined circumstances affecting test execution; typical actions are *"go"* (continue), *"no-go"* (cease test), or *"hold"* (delay).

Gray Box. Description of a hybrid test approach that combines the beneficial aspects of *white* and *black box* approaches, providing the test team with limited insight into the inner workings of the system.

Ground equipment. A general term to describe all non-flying support systems that enable flight of the *air vehicle* or *system under test*, which may or may not be part of it. For the military, also called *support equipment*, and further segregated into *common* (shared among two or more air vehicles) or *peculiar* (unique to one platform).

Ground test. Related to lab test in that ground test is a precursor to flight test; however, a *ground test* typically indicates a fully integrated system within the air vehicle, ready in most aspects for flight test as the next step in development.

Hangar. Generally, the shelter for the tested system when not being used; often leased, rented, or borrowed when not owned by the test organization and must be accounted for in test planning and execution.

Hypothesis. Propositions describing the modes, processes, or interactions that explain physical observations, provisionally adopted to guide investigation through the *scientific method*.

Information. Compiled data that describe, identify, or define the particular performance characteristic(s) of the *system under test*.

Instrumentation. Equipment, hardware, software, or sensors used to take measurements of the *system under test* when subjected to the desired environment and inputs, internal or external to the air vehicle or system

Insight. See **Wisdom**.

Instrumentation List. A detailed account of all internal and external data sources with particular regard to data rate, frequency, range, accuracy, recording method, and parameter category (SOF, SOT, AC).

Interim Report. A summary of results, conclusions, and recommendations delivered to the program sponsor during test execution. An interim is (by definition) followed up with the final test report at the end of the test program.

Interpolation. Projection of system performance inside of the bounds of collected test data. An assumption of how the performance varies between known test points guides *interpolation*; thus, the closer they are to the desired point, the higher the accuracy and certainty. *Interpolation* also requires an assumption that the data behave smoothly (no discontinuities). Generally, *interpolation* is the preferred method of determining system performance. See **Extrapolation**.

Key Performance Parameter (KPP). Expression of a fundamental performance value essential for providing desired capability, i.e., successful operations doubtful unless the system provides performance level stipulated by *KPP*. For design trade space, where applicable, a *KPP* often is expressed with *threshold* and *objective* values.

Knock-it-off. Pilot-speak for stopping dynamic maneuvering and returning aircraft to a stable, static condition. The phrase can have several other meanings depending on context:

1) Formation maneuvering: Stop the engagement and separate the aircraft.
2) Test event: Stop taking data and recover aircraft before reaching a limit, e.g., attitude, airspeed, altitude).
3) Test flight: Complete data taking and return to base for landing.

Knowledge. Two definitions:

1) Understanding regarding performance characteristics, requirements compliance, effectiveness, or suitability of the system based on collected data and assembled information, often from additional analysis.
2) Understanding the basic tenets, fundamentals, practices, issues, and concerns regarding the art and science of flight test planning, execution, and reporting. One gains *knowledge* through instruction and study.

Laboratory/Lab test. Generally, not directly part of the flight test, as lab testing involves a non-integrated system (not installed within the air vehicle). However, *lab testing* is an integral part of gaining knowledge and insight regarding the system performance and is a stepping stone toward flight tests.

Lessons Learned. Observations, comments, corrections that an organization gathers regarding its operations and processes, which can then be folded back into improving the organization.

Limitation to Scope. Restriction placed on the test program driven by cost, schedule, or residual risk considerations; results in conclusions and recommendations with restricted/curtailed operational applicability.

Measure/Measurement. To obtain dimensional information (e.g., distance, time, rates, accelerations, power) of the **system under test** to compare to expectations (for requirements compliance or evaluation)

Met. Statement of fact regarding the **system under test**, as compared to the specification during verification: system performance was equal to that which was specified.

Mission Impact (MI). The beneficial or detrimental effect that a system behavior, characteristics, or level of performance has on the ability to conduct the primary or secondary mission or task assigned to that system. The *MI* provides the **So What?** for the evaluation and is a vital part of the test report.

Mission Relation (MR). An expression of how a particular system characteristic directly or indirectly influences mission or task success. The system characteristic may have a beneficial or detrimental *MR*. Some observable or measurable characteristics do not have an *MR*.

Mission System Description (MSD). A technical discussion of one or more of the sensor systems on the air vehicle, including software and hardware, signal paths, and command and control relationships.

Mission. The aviation, navigation, communication, sensing, command, control, or another useful task the operator desires to perform; the end state capability or effect that the system acquires, achieves, or assists the end-user in obtaining.

Navigate/navigation. The actions and processes involved in directing an air vehicle in flight from the current location to the desired location.

No-Vote. Test execution concept whereby all members of the test team are obligated to verbally request a stop to test when conditions exist that potentially adversely affect the safety of the test. The *no-vote* stays in effect until those conditions are corrected or explained such that they no longer are a hazard/threat, real or perceived.

Objective. Upper bound value for a requirement intended to indicate Operator's perception of value for increased performance and provide design trade space for optimization against cost/schedule constraints.

Observer effect. In physics, this means that there are changes to the item under observation made by the act of observation. For a flight test, the FTE must carefully consider the impact of instrumentation and test method on the system characteristics being measured, verified, or validated. The *observer effect* is related to the **uncertainty principle**.

Operational Countdown. Step-by-step listing of actions required to get to the test, typically given days, hours, and minutes to go for each step with person or role responsible for each.

Operational Test & Evaluation (OT&E). Test performed after DT&E intended to "validate that the *system under test* can effectively execute its mission in a realistic operational environment when operated by typical operators against representative threats."[7]

Operator. See *End-user*.

Performance Baseline. Description of the system created by listing individual quantifiable outcomes (measures) the system must provide to meet the user's overall capability need (system engineering).

Precautionary Measure (PM). Additional test team action, procedure, or process (or modification of one previously proposed) included in the test plan and intended to disassociate the cause and hazard, reducing risk likelihood.

Prediction. Expected test outcome given known inputs and controlled environment based on engineering analysis of the system, design intent, and requirements (specifications).

Project Management. The required resource, personnel, infrastructure, and schedule details necessary for successful test execution. The *project management* section of the test plan guides the team through the effort with the names, contact information, and details. An essential part of this is expectation management, represented by an agreement in the test plan for the format and frequency of the resulting test reports.

Qualitative. Description of the system performance based on non-numeric performance measurements comprising observations and comments, either subjective or objective.

Quantitative. Description of the system performance based on numerical data collected during the test, primarily objective and relative to known truth reference data.

Question. The item(s) of interest that prompted the initiation of the test program, such as (1) assessing usefulness, usability, and maturity of the design, (2) determining compliance with requirements, or (3) evaluating the effectiveness and suitability of a system concerning an intended mission or task.

---

[7] Per DT&E definition, Defense Acquisition University https://dap.dau.mil/acquipedia, retrieved September 3, 2016.

Quicklook. A report containing results, conclusions, and recommendations about a very narrow area of performance, typically presented to the program manager after a particular test flight or phase of testing that was investigating one characteristic, topic, or task for the *system under test*. Often, a *Quicklook* includes a face-to-face presentation along with a written document, which enables detailed discussion.

Recommendation. The final step in the test reporting process, which informs the reader of the test team's appraisal of the best course of action for further development of the *system under test*. The *recommendation* connects the test data to the decision and facilitates the *decision-quality data* goal of the flight test.

Referred data. See *Generalized data*.

Regression test. A subset of testing (lab, ground, or flight) that concentrates on determining whether complete system functionality and operational capability remains after making a change to the system. In other words, *regression test* checks whether the system was inadvertently "broken" in any way after "fixing" it.

Repeatability. Essential requirement for test execution and the basis of the need for test documentation. *Repeatability* allows for follow-on testing to *verify* corrections, *regression testing* of functionality, and to *evaluate* improvements.

Requirement. "A singular documented physical and functional need that a particular design, product, or process must be able to perform... identifies a necessary attribute, capability, characteristic, or quality of a system for it to have value and utility to a customer, organization, internal user, or other stakeholder."[8]

Residual risk. After the application of the precautionary measure(s) and corrective action(s), residual risk is the assessment of the hazard (probability and consequence). Test plan approval virtually accepts the residual risk on behalf of the test organization.

---

[8] Wikipedia contributors. (n.d.). *Requirements*. In Wikipedia, The Free Encyclopedia. Retrieved September 3, 2016, from https://en.wikipedia.org/wiki/Requirement

Result. Fact, data, or information gained from a test (*quantitative* or *qualitative*) used for comparison to requirements (*verification*) or as the basis of a conclusion (*evaluation*) on a system performance characteristic.

Risk. Expression of loss in terms of likelihood of occurrence and severity of consequence; the test planning process is primarily interested in *risk* due to the demands of the test program.

Risk Management. The application of numerical ratings or value judgment to the weighing of risks against the controls necessary to minimize these risks. A *risk management* process follows the generic flow:

1) **Risk Identification**: locate the **hazards** and determine where risks lie within the operating envelope, test process, or expected conditions

2) **Risk Analysis**: develop an understanding of the risk, as defined by the dimensions of probability and consequence.

3) **Risk Mitigation**: determine appropriate **precautionary measure(s)** and **corrective action(s)** to reduce the risk to an acceptable level

4) **Implement Controls**: put the selected measures in place, for flight test, this means to insert the measure(s) and action(s) into the test **scope** and **method** (i.e., not optional, but part of test execution).

5) **Monitor**: Observe the results of measure(s) and action(s) to ensure they are achieving desired outcomes, in flight test this is supported by post-event debrief, lessons learned, THA process, and that *no-vote*.

Safe. Regarding the aim of the test planning process, the degree to which test **risk management** techniques and practices are used by the test team to reduce the **residual risk** and eliminate/avoid/control test **hazards**.

Safety Checklist (SC). Test planning tool in use by NAVAIR to ensure that test teams throughout the organization thoroughly consider selected safety-related issues. The *SC* does not provide the answers to the issues; instead, it forms an internal index to direct the reader to the discussion in the test plan.

Safety of Flight (SOF). Instrumentation category to indicate that verified correct operation and real-time visibility of the parameter is required during all phases of flight of **air vehicle** or **system under test**.

Safety of Test (SOT). Instrumentation category to indicate that verified correct operation and real-time visibility of the parameter is required during specific named test events of *air vehicle* or *system under test*.

Scientific Method. A guide for experimentation and exploration in science, instrumental in the development of theories and descriptions of the natural world around us, and a useful framework for discovery and analysis of human-made systems.

Signature Page. For the test plan, the signature page is a means to enforce test discipline. The *signature page* requires individuals who join the test in execution to review and understand the plan, then sign to indicate compliance.

Skill. Recognized *ability* and *knowledge* routinely and accurately applied to the science and art of test planning, execution, and reporting; gained from experience and practice in the field.

Specification/Spec. "An explicit set of requirements to be satisfied by a material, product, system, or service;"[9] developed through the system engineering process and the principle document for use in requirements compliance testing (*verification*).

Standard Day. Conditions used by the International Civil Aviation Organization (ICAO) for comparing all aircraft and engine performance. The primary standard day conditions are:

1. temperature, 15 °C or 52 °F
2. altitude, mean sea level
3. pressure, 29.92 inches of mercury

Standard Operating Procedure (SOP). A document provided by an organization's leader expressing desired/required actions based on situations; essentially, the leader's guide for the conduct of the group.

Status Report. Provided by the test team to the test program sponsor during any of the test phases (planning, execution, or reporting) to give an appraisal

---

[9] Form and Style of Standards, ASTM Blue Book, http://www.astm.org/COMMIT/Blue_Book.pdf, American Society for Testing and Materials (ASTM), 2012, retrieved September 3, 2016.

of current issues, problems, concerns, or progress. A *status report* does not contain test **results**, **conclusions**, or system-related **recommendations**.

Success Criteria. Summation of conditions, data, and information that must be collected or determined during a test event for the test team to declare completion of the test objectives to an acceptable level.

Suitability/Suitable. Statement of system usefulness in achieving desired outcomes. *Suitability* encompasses concepts such as reliability, availability, maintainability, and supportability (the "*-ilities*").

System Under Test. The component, assembly, subsystem, hardware, or software that is the subject of the test and evaluation effort. The *system under test* may be a single piece of equipment or software integrated into an air vehicle, or it may be the entire ***air vehicle***.

Test. An event where the system or air vehicle is subjected to a controlled environment with known inputs to allow for observation of the outputs and system response.

Test and Test Conditions (T&TC). Table that provides test name, conditions and tolerances, variables, priority, test phases, residual risk (from THA), and an indication of the method (by name or title).

Test Director (TD). A qualified and designated individual who typically performs test coordination duties. Other names for the *TD* may include coordinator, lead FTE, team lead, or some other variant.

Test Execution. The process of performing the test method described in the test plan for the ***system under test*** according to the test scope. *Test execution* only occurs after successful test planning and is always accompanied by test reporting.

Test Hazard Analysis (THA). Three unique definitions/usages:

1. An analysis to identify **hazards** associated with the test design and implement measures and actions to reduce test risk. The *THA* is a foundational part of test **risk management**.

2. A table that provides *hazard* identification, mitigation, and *residual risk* categorization. The table presentation often is segregated by the test phase, test name, or test event.

3. An individual result from the *THA* process (first usage above), which identifies (1) a single, specific *hazard*, (2) the planned *precautionary measures* or *corrective actions* relative to that hazard, and (3) the *residual risk* category. The *THAs* are typically read verbatim at the pre-event briefing.

Test Matrix. See **Test & Test Conditions**.

Test Plan. Documented test team thought process regarding (1) what question they are attempting to answer, (2) how they intend to answer it, and (3) how to ensure the test is conducted *safely*, *efficiently*, and *effectively*.

Test Readiness Review (TRR). A deliberate determination that the *system under test* is ready to proceed to a phase of testing. The considers evidence from many sources, including maintenance, system maturity, results of previous testing, and risk analysis (particularly *THA*).

Test Report. The result of the test effort is to provide decision-quality data to someone to make a development or acquisition decision. Test serves to reduce risk and clarify assumptions by determining facts about the system's performance and design. The *Test Report* is how those facts are conveyed to a decision-maker, either in engineering design, sustainment, operations, or program management.

Test Triangle. An analysis concept to remind the FTE that a test result by itself does not necessarily reflect system performance, but must be viewed first through the lens of instrumentation/set-up and test procedure/method. Once those two areas are understood, then the result may be assigned to system performance.

Threshold. Lower bound value for a requirement intended to indicate the *Operator's* minimum acceptable value and bound design trade space for optimization against cost/schedule constraints.

Unreferred data. Once *generalized* or *referred*, data is then transferred to desired (or operationally representative) conditions, resulting in the performance values obtained if the test team performed the test under desired conditions.

User. See *Operator.*

Validate/Validation. A level of flight test where the objectives include an assessment of a system's effectiveness and suitability for a particular mission or task to determine whether the system provides the desired capability.

Verify/Verification. A level of flight test where the objectives include an assessment of system performance and comparison against the design criteria resulting in an understanding of spec compliance and whether the system was built right.

White Box. Description of test approach where the test team has complete insight into the inner workings of the system and, therefore, can fully understand the signal path and data flow while testing system response.

Wisdom. The goal of flight test is to collect data, assemble information, and generate knowledge. *Wisdom* is the decision-quality data conveyed to program management to support fully-informed, risk-based decision-making regarding cost/schedule/performance tradeoffs during system design, development, fielding, and sustainment. The purpose of flight test is to plan and execute tests and evaluations that culminate in documented *wisdom* (in the form of the test report) to manage a system, process, program, or capability.

Acronym List

AC	Analysis Critical
ALFS	Advanced Low-Frequency Sonar
ASTM	American Society for Testing and Materials
CA	Corrective Action
CISL	College of Interdisciplinary Studies and Leadership (NAVAIR)
CLIO	College of Logistics and Industrial Operations (NAVAIR)
CM	Configuration Management
CONEMP	Concept of Employment
CONOPS	Concept of Operations
COTF	Commander, Operational Test Forces (US Navy)
CPM	College of Program Management (NAVAIR)
CT	Contractor Test
CT&E	College of Test & Evaluation (NAVAIR)
DMOT	Detailed Method of Test
DT	Developmental Test
DT&E	Developmental Test & Evaluation
ESM	Electronic Surveillance Measures
FAA	Federal Aviation Administration
FC	Flight Clearance
FCD	Flight Control Description
FRR	Flight Readiness Review
FTE	Flight Test Engineer
GFTD	Government Flight Test Director
GPS	Global Positioning System
GSE	Ground Support Equipment
GW	Gross Weight
IFF	Identification Friend or Foe
INS	Inertial Navigation System
JSF	Joint Strike Fighter
KAS	Knowledge, Ability, Skill
KPP	Key Performance Parameter
M&S	Modeling and Simulation
MI	Mission Impact
MR	Mission Relation
MSD	Mission System Description

NAS	Naval Air Station
NAVAIR	Naval Air System Command (US Navy)
NFO	Naval Flight Officer
OFP	Operational Flight Program
OT	Operational Test
OT&E	Operational Test & Evaluation
OTD	Operational Test Director
PM	Precautionary Measure or Program Manager
SAR	Search and Rescue
SC	Safety Checklist
SOF	Safety of Flight
SOP	Standard Operating Procedure
SOT	Safety of Test
STOVL	Short Take-off/Vertical Landing
T&E	Test and Evaluation
T&TC	Test and Test Conditions
TBD	To Be Determined
TCAS	Terminal Collision Avoidance System
TD	Test Director
THA	Test Hazard Analysis
TOC	Table of Contents
TP	Test Planning or Test Plan
TPS	Test Pilot School (US Navy)
TR	Test Reporting or Test Report
TRR	Test Readiness Review
UA	Unacceptable
UAS	Unmanned Aerial System
UAV	Unmanned Aerial Vehicle
USMC	United States Marine Corps
V/STOL	Vertical/Short Take-off and Landing
VTOL	Vertical Take-off and Landing
W&B	Weight and Balance
XP	Experimental Pilot (US Army)

Photo Credits

Note: The appearance of U.S. Department of Defense (DoD) visual information does not imply or constitute DoD endorsement.

Figure 1, Page 4: Otto Lilienthal

Otto Lilienthal was flying in Germany in 1893. He controlled the aircraft by kicking, extending, and bending his legs to change the glider's center of gravity. Photo from http://www.wright-brothers. org/History_Wing/History_of_the_Airplane/Century_Before/ Century_Before_Intro/Century_Before_ Intro.htm, retrieved 5 Sept 2016.

Figure 2, Page 6: Lockheed Martin F-35 Lightning II JSF

Lt. Cmdr. Daniel "Tonto" Kitts, an F-35 Lightning II test pilot assigned to the Salty Dogs of Air Test and Evaluation Squadron (VX) 23, landed in the history books Feb. 10, 2016, when he performed the first arrestment of an F-35C with external weapons. Flight 282 of aircraft CF-03 from the F-35 Lightning II Patuxent River Integrated Test Force (ITF) was based at NAS Patuxent River, Md. (U.S. Navy photo courtesy of Dane Wiedmann). Photo retrieved on Jan 9, 2020, from https://www.defense.gov/observe/photogallery/ igphoto/2001556447/

Figure 3, Page 8: North American XB-70A Valkyrie

ED97-44244-2 This photo shows XB-70A #1 taking off on a research flight, escorted by a TB-58 chase plane. The TB-58, a prototype B-58, modified as a trainer, had a dash speed of Mach 2. This allowed it to stay close to the XB-70 as it conducted its research maneuvers. When the XB-70 was flying at or near Mach 3, the slower TB-58 could often keep up with it by flying lower and cutting inside the turns in the XB-70's flight path when these occurred. (1960s NASA Pho-to/North American photo). Photo from https://www. nasa.gov/centers/dryden/multimedia/imagegallery/XB-70/ED97-44244-2. html

Figure 4, Page 10: Lockheed Martin MH-60R Seahawk

A U.S. Navy MH-60R Seahawk with Helicopter Maritime Strike Squadron 78 (HSM-78) "Blue Hawks" flies over Lake Huron, Mich. during a Northern Strike 19 training mission on July 26, 2019. (U.S. Air National Guard photo by Master Sgt. Matt Hecht). Photo retrieved on Jan 9, 2020, from https://www.dvidshub. net/image/5620303/us-navy-seahawks-train-during-northern-strike-19

Figure 5, Page 27: Thales AN/ASQ-22 ALFS Transducer Array
The Folding Light Acoustic System for Helicopter (FLASH), designed and built by the Thales Group, was modified for use with the US Navy's MH-60R Multi-Mission Helicopter. Photo ©2016 The Thales Group, retrieved from https://www.thalesgroup.com/en on 4 Sept 2016. Used by permission.

Figure 7, Page 35: Bell AH-1W Cobra
Author's photo, taken by Robert Cole (2002). The photo was taken while flying the test aircraft over the beach at Panama City, FL, to the test range to evaluate the ability to shoot submerged sea mines. The author is in the front (gunner's) seat.

Figure 8, Page 36: Bell/Boeing V-22 Osprey
170619-N-ZI646-067 BISMARCK SEA (June 19, 2017) - An MV-22 Osprey, assigned to the "Dragons" of Marine Medium Tiltrotor Squadron (VMM) 265 Reinforced, lifts off from the flight deck of the amphibious assault ship USS Bonhomme Richard (LHD 6). Bonhomme Richard, the flagship of the Bonhomme Richard Expeditionary Strike Group (ESG), is operating in the Indo-Asia-Pacific region to enhance partnerships and be a ready-response force for any type of contingency. (U.S. Navy photo by Mass Communication Specialist 1st Class James Mitchell/Released). Photo retrieved on Jan 9, 2020, from: https://www.dvidshub.net/image/3497351/uss-bonhomme-richard-operations

Figure 9, Page 41: Lockheed AH-56 Cheyenne
By William Pretrina, posted initially at http://flickr.com/photos/83969498@N02/7757082888, licensed under the terms of Creative Commons Attribution 2.0 Generic license (CC-by-2.0), https://creativecommons.org/licenses/by/2.0/deed.en, no changes/alterations to original were made.

Figure 10, Page 42: Lockheed Martin MH-60R Seahawk
PACIFIC OCEAN (Dec. 2, 2019) An MH-60R Seahawk, assigned to the "Wolf Pack" of Helicopter Maritime Strike Squadron (HSM 75), takes off from the flight deck of the Arleigh Burke-class guided-missile destroyer USS Kidd (DDG 100) Dec. 2, 2019. Kidd is underway conducting routine training in the Eastern Pacific Ocean. (U.S. Navy photo by Mass Communication Specialist 3rd Class Brandie Nuzzi). Photo retrieved on Jan 9, 2020, from https://www.dvidshub.net/image/5955568/uss-kidd-ddg-100

Figure 11, Page 47: Northrup Grumman E-2D Advanced Haw-keye
180725-N-RG171-0150 ATLANTIC OCEAN (July 25, 2018) An E-2D Hawkeye assigned to the Bluetails of Carrier Airborne Early Warning Squadron (VAW) 121 prepares to land on the flight deck aboard the Nimitz-class aircraft carrier USS Abraham Lincoln (CVN 72). (U.S. Navy photo by Mass Communication Specialist Seaman Will Hardy/Released). Photo retrieved on Jan 9, 2020, from https://www.dvidshub.net/image/4590688/180725-n-rg171-0150

Figure 13, Page 90: Northrup Grumman MQ-8B Fire Scout
190626-N-QI061-0445 ATLANTIC OCEAN (June 26, 2019) An MQ-8B Fire Scout assigned to the Sea Knights of Helicopter Sea Combat Squadron (HSC) 22 takes off from the flight deck of the Freedom-class littoral combat ship USS Milwaukee (LCS 5). (U.S. Navy photo by Mass Communication Specialist 3rd Class Nathan T. Beard/Released). Photo retrieved on Jan 9, 2020, from https://www.dvidshub.net/image/5541528/190626-n-qi061-0445

Index

Printed in the United States
By Bookmasters